Rocky & Jean,

Thank you so m
for helping make this
dream a reality. We
so enjoy you both and
your family and look
forward to getting to know
you better.
            Blessings,
                A.J.

Finding Father

Finding Father

a journey into the loving arms of Daddy God

A.J. Jones
foreword by John Arnott

Published by XP Publishing
A department of Christian Services Association
P.O. Box 1017, Maricopa, Arizona 85139
United States of America
www.XPpublishing.com

ISBN-13: 978-1-936101-37-5

Printed in The United States of America. For Worldwide Distribution

DEDICATION

John and Carol, the words "thank you" and "I love you" seem so inadequate to express my deepest sentiments. You have demonstrated God's heart to me so thoroughly and so consistently. Thank you for being key people in His faithful plan to love me back to life.

To the many others along the way that have parented me, encouraged me, believed in me, loved me and been a friend to me in dark times and great times: I thank you. Fred & Sharon, Connie and Jeremy, Ian and Janice, Aunt Joani and Uncle Paul – thank you for being God's arms extended. Janna, thanks for not giving up on me; you are amazing. Stuart and Lynley, Jenni, Sarah, Cathy and Gordon, your faithfulness is overwhelming.

Leilani, thank you for all you do for us. We could not do what we do, if you were not there helping us do it. Thanks for being so awesome with the girls, for editing, and for making my life easier.

Thank you to my Grace Center family: Jeff & Becky, you are incredible leaders; to the great staff that make working at Grace so much fun; to our emanate family – you guys are awesome; and to everyone who helped make this book a reality - thank you so much.

Patricia King, thank you. It's amazing how the Lord intersects us at pivotal moments to move me to the next point. You have been such a blessing for many years.

Carol Martinez, you are a star. It has been an absolute pleasure to work with you and XP Publishing. Thank you for working so hard to get this book out on time. You have the patience of a saint!

Mom, Suey, Scott and Evan, I love you more than I can communicate and pray you continue on your quest to find your home in Him.

Dad, I miss you.

Abi and Tia, mommy is so proud of you. I love you so much it hurts. The Lord has taught me so much about His heart and unconditional love for His kids through loving you. I pray everyday to represent His heart toward you well, and for grace and healing for the moments when I fail.

Alyn, you are one of God's greatest gifts to me. I cannot imagine a world without you in it. You are my best friend, and a wonderful husband and father. I love living this adventure with you. Thank you for all your help with this book; all the writing, encouragement, and looking after the kids while I struggled to get words on paper. You really are the best. I love you!

ENDORSEMENTS

"Written in bite size chewable pieces, this is a great meal served up by AJ Jones, ready to be devoured by souls hungry for the truth about having a transparent relationship with God. Practical and amazing insights are contained in this inspiring training tool. This book has the potential to transform lives and help you establish a strong foundation for His Kingdom's sake. Just great!"

James W. Goll - Encounter Network

"Through this powerful devotional journey, AJ leads us right into the center of the Father's heart to a place of deep security and rest in His love. Qualified to lead, because she has first found her own way home to His heart, AJ presents biblical insights and lessons which allow us to explode the roadblocks in our pathway toward the Father. As one who has walked with Father 65 years, I still found, through her book, a new vitality and fresh intimacy with Him. Thank you, AJ. Through AJ's book many will, at last, find that heart connection that has been missing. You will love this practical biblical help."

Betsy and Chester Kylstra - Restoring the Foundations

"After I read through *Finding Father*, I wanted all my family and staff to read it and activate the principles. Everyone needs an initial revelation of Father's Love, but it is also good for us to be renewed in it over the years. If you have never received a revelation of Father's love, you will when you read this book. If you need your revelation renewed, you will have your desire fulfilled. I find AJ's book, *Finding Father*, both encouraging and enlightening. It can be used for personal Bible study or for group study. Journey through the book... you will find Him."

Patricia King - XPmedia

"AJ Jones, a spiritual daughter to me, lives and practices the principles that she so clearly shares in her book. I highly recommend that you make this book part of your daily devotional life. It will change you from the inside out and bring you into an intimate relationship with the Father, the Son and the Holy Spirit."

Carol Arnott - Founding Pastor, TACF

Testimonies from people who have worked through the material:

"This study into the Father heart of God offers significant spiritual and practical insight into the true nature of God. Each week the Word comes to life and touches the heart in ways that produce truth for the lies so many of us believe about God. AJ has expressed her journey so candidly that one cannot help but relate on so many levels. The honesty and sincerity in which this study is written clearly communicates the Father heart of God. After working through this study I find myself walking in a greater level of trust and rest, living each day with a renewed hope and assurance of God as my Father, and what that means from a purely practical place."

S. Singleton

"Through the teaching presented in this course I have learned just how much Father God loves me. I often call him Abba, but the revelation that He is just like my earthly father in His affections toward me did not register until taking this class. After one of the Wednesday night sessions it dawned on me, hey, he really loves me just like my Dad - who would do anything for me and who loves me no matter what. This is HUGE for me because I am a perfectionist and very hard on myself when I make mistakes. Knowing His love allows me to relax in His presence and in relationship with my Abba - I am learning what it means to abide, and it's lovely!!!"

T. Price

"This Father Heart study has been pivotal in my relationship with the Lord. AJ does a wonderful job of revealing the truth about our Father in heaven and uprooting the ungodly beliefs we have believed for so long. Through her study I fell in love with the Lord all over again, but on a new foundation of truth. The transformation of my heart toward the Father has brought me freedom that I never knew existed. This has changed everything."

"I have gained confidence, security, and an increase of faith. The way I relate and spend time with the Lord is totally different and is something that I look forward to. My thoughts about myself and about my Father are positive, and are birthing life instead of death."

A. Harris

"We can know God as Creator, Savior and Eternal God but without a knowledge of the intimate love of His father's heart, we lose out of an entire facet of His being; the part that tenderly loves us and fiercely protects us. AJ's teaching on the Father's Heart has again reminded me that, backed with His perfect love, I can live boldly, free of fear and full of hope! And just as importantly, I can believe this for my family."

K. Hallum

TABLE OF CONTENTS

Week Four

Week Five

Week Six

Week Seven

Week Twelve

FOREWORD

It is rare that I get to write a foreword to a book that teaches truths and principles that I totally love and believe in. And it is all the more special when that book is written by someone who is a spiritual daughter to Carol and me. We have known Allyson (A J) since 1991 when a friend brought her kicking and screaming to our then little church at the end of the runway in Toronto. She cried and wailed all through the meeting and in the end, fell sobbing into my arms. That day, she began her own personal journey of Finding Father It was and is her Heavenly Father as revealed through Jesus Christ, that transformed her life from a deeply wounded teenager, who didn't want to live anymore, into a vibrant, capable woman of God who has been revolutionized by the very things she is wanting to share, dear reader, with you. It thrills me now to see her, along with Alyn her husband, leading a group of hundreds of young adults into the very things that transformed her life. There is nothing so powerful as biblical truth that is brought forth from the heart of one that has been totally transformed by the very teaching they share. It "rings true." It feels right. It ministers to the deep places of the heart and soul. It enlightens the mind. Such is this book, *Finding Father*.

Allow AJ to take you, step by step, day by day, through these powerful life-changing lessons. If you do it, it will transform you. If you do it, you will fall deeper in love with your Savior and your Creator. If you do it, not only will you and your family enjoy the "new you" but you will be equipped and empowered to share with many others that which I believe is essential to freedom in Christ. You will be walking in God's love and then giving it away to a broken, needy world around you, and many of them are your family and friends. Oh, and don't plan to speed-read this book. This work is for the heart, and the heart is a slow learner. Some things are not instant fast food, and this is one of those. Get ready to meet your Father!

John Arnott, Founding Pastor,
Catch the Fire Toronto and
Partners in Harvest

HOW TO USE THIS BOOK

The *Finding Father* Study Guide is a valuable tool for you to truly know your Heavenly Father's heart for you. The Guide is perfectly suited for an individual to use during their daily devotion time, but is also a valuable resource for group Bible Studies.

For Personal Use

1. Read through the daily lesson notes. Meditate on the Scriptures and the principles. Look up the Scriptures in your own Bible and underline.
2. Read through the Lesson Reflections and Applications and engage in the applications.
3. Journal. Write down any significant insights Father is revealing to you.
4. Most weeks there are only five days worth of "study" per week. On the additional days I encourage you to go back and spend more time reflecting and engaging with heaven over the days that seem most pertinent to you.

For Bible Study Use

1. Each student in the Study has this guide and should follow the above stated personal study guidelines. The Bible Study Instructor initially teaches the Introduction Lesson for each week to the class. The instructor also might want to give an overview for the week ahead based on the daily lessons. Open the class for discussion.
2. Invite the group to follow the guide each day and take notes of significant things the Lord is saying to them.
3. When they return the next week, review the week's lessons and invite the group to share their testimonies, questions, and insights.
4. Have a prayer and ministry time at the end of the session.

You will also be developing and strengthening two new skill sets as you work through this study: journaling and soaking. I encourage you to make time each day to do the exercises that follow each day's teaching and then spend at least 20 – 30 minutes soaking. While the teaching starts to feed your brain and maybe even rewrite some truth for you, the journaling and soaking times are what will write that new revelation to your heart. I can honestly say that about 80% of the healing of the heart I have received has come from these times of engaging with heaven and letting God be God and do the surgery that needs to be done. Don't skip it or allow it to be just a mental assent. Invite the Holy Spirit to come and meet with you and deliver to your heart the revelation of the Father Heart of God.

WELCOME TO THE JOURNEY!

By reading this study guide and engaging in the applications, you are embarking on a journey into the heart of Father God for you. This journey will launch you into an exciting, new, grace-filled season in your life! Much of the revelation I share in this guide has come through walking out the healing process in my own life while resting in the hands of our wonderful Daddy God. Man, what a journey it has been!

Like many of you, I had heard teaching for years on "the Father Heart of God," but somehow I still managed to miss most of what God was trying to speak to me. I continued to live life as if I had to struggle on my own. I continued to strive, compete and earn love as though this was what I was born to do. I lived as though it was God's master plan for me to strive and fight tooth and nail every day to remain in a place of not striving in order to insure that I was loved. I know striving to not strive is fairly silly, but we do it so often and don't even realize it – at least I didn't.

See, here's the thing: we need to start dealing with our junk; the emotional baggage we have been carrying around for longer than any of us can remember, and let God have it. I began to realize the reason I didn't feel loved and couldn't approach a loving God was because the reality of the negative experiences and messages of my past seemed more real than the reality of Scripture. So, while I could hear that I was loved a thousand times and then a thousand more, I would still miss that reality because everything within me screamed it was a lie. It wasn't my intention to argue with God (especially knowing that no one who does so ever wins), but life had jumped up and bit me enough times that I did. I had no grid for a loving God, no matter how much I really wanted to believe it.

This journey will launch you into an exciting, new, grace-filled season... walking out the healing process... while resting in the hands of our wonderful Daddy God.

Maybe you are like I was – desperately wanting to live in the reality of Papa God's love, but so hedged in by your own walls that you believe there is no way out. I have news for you: God knows. He knows all your fears, your pain, everything you carry. He understands all your walls and He will be just as faithful to you as He has been to me. How do I know? Because He brought me out of the miry place and taught me to rest in His love. If He can do it for me He will do it for you!

What is the cause of our walls?

You may wonder, "What caused my walls?" The answer applies to everyone: Life. Our closed off places are most often formed by life's experiences. As children and even adults, it is very easy to blame others for the way our lives have turned out. We rarely want to take responsibility for our reactions to what happened to us or for the state of heart and mind we find ourselves in today. It would be much easier to say, "It's all Dad's fault that I'm the way I am," or "Mom should have loved me more," but the fact remains that in most cases, they have done their best as well. No parent ever intentionally sets out to hurt his or her own child. They don't gleefully plan the hours of counseling it will take to undo the way they brought us up. Many times, they are just doing the very best they can with what they have. You have probably experienced some wonderful moments growing up that you will cherish as a family for a lifetime, and yet there might also be moments that you will spend your lifetime trying to forget.

Someone very wise once said, "I lurting people hurt people." That seems to put it all in perspective. Neither your parents nor my parents had perfect lives before their children were born.

Someone very wise once said, "Hurting people hurt people." That seems to put it all in perspective for me. Neither your parents nor my parents had perfect lives before their children were born. They have been through pain, fear, disappointment, betrayal, and maybe even abuse. And if they haven't worked through those things with Jesus and had His healing touch restore their hearts, then they continue to carry those hurts. As I said, hurting people hurt people. It's not about casting blame; it's about realizing that we have all hurt other people: our family, friends, colleagues, pastors and so on. There is an interesting verse in Scripture that often stops me short when I am in danger of judging others:

I therefore have no excuse, everyone of you who passes judgment, for in that which you judge another, you condemn yourself, for you who judge practice the same things. (Romans 2:1)

There are many of us that are still so busy blaming our parents for the wrong in our lives that we almost don't have a life. What's ironic is that often the very things we criticized our parents for are the same things that we ourselves are doing! Scary how true Scripture is, isn't it? At some point in our development we need to realize that life is made up of events and our reactions to those events. Life is made up of choices. We need to start taking responsibility for our part of the deal – for our reactions and our choices. Then, we need to let God heal those choices as well as the consequences that we didn't have control over. You and I are not meant to live overshadowed by our past. We are promised "life and life more abundant," however, we rarely live in that reality.

Getting started!

So, how do we start? It begins with letting God dig in our gardens and root out the weeds, so to speak. What that means is simply letting God love us back to life by first removing the lies we have believed, lifting the pain that has crushed us, pulling out the roots of betrayal and disappointment and then pruning us back so our lives can begin to flourish with new growth.

It begins with letting God dig in our gardens and root out the weeds, so to speak. What that means is simply letting God love us back to life.

I know it doesn't sound pleasant, and perhaps even now you are wondering if you can return the book for a refund or an exchange on a fiction that you can hide in. I have been in that same place, my friend, and I can't blame you for feeling that way – but the reality is that once the last page of the fiction is done, life comes right back up to bite you again. I challenge you to bite it back!

Let's start dealing with the baggage that needs to be dealt with, and believe that God actually does want to heal, restore and set us free! What happens after that? We find that we are living life knowing we are fully loved and accepted. We discover that we can greet each day with a "Good Morning Father! Let the day begin!" We learn that when life hurts us we have a safe place in Father's arms to rest and be restored. We find Home.

HEARING GOD'S VOICE

One of the great benefits of being a son or daughter of God is the ability to hear His voice. This is a birthright gift! Under the Old Covenant, God spoke mostly to His prophets only, but under the New Covenant, God speaks to all of His children (Acts 2:17). If you are a born again believer, you can hear God's voice! What a wonderful blessing!

My journey into hearing God's voice was a slow one; mainly because I didn't understand how God spoke. It was also because I feared opening up to hearing God's voice as it had a "New Age" sound to it. Only after I studied the Scriptures did I understand that God wanted to speak to me personally. However understanding that God wants to speak to you and learning how to hear his voice are different things! My biggest breakthrough came after hearing Dr. Mark Virkler teach his "Communion with God" course many years ago. Much of the material in this chapter is based on his excellent teaching.

Jesus modeled life for us perfectly. He came to earth to save us, yes, but also to show us how to live a life in sync with our Heavenly Father.

In John 12:50, Jesus makes this incredible statement:

Whatever I say is just what the Father has told me to say. (NIV)

Think about that for a moment. That's a profound statement. Jesus is declaring to the people that whatever He says, the Father told Him to say. Here you have an inside glimpse into Jesus' relationship with His Father - He took time to hear (Luke:5.16) what His Father was saying before He said anything.

Under the new covenant, God speaks to all of His children. If you are a born again believer, you can hear God's voice!

In a similar verse, John 5:19, Jesus says,

The Son can do nothing by Himself; He can do only what He sees His Father doing. (NIV)

Jesus, by supernatural sight, sees what His Father is doing and does likewise.

If Jesus, the very Son of God, needed to hear from His Father before He could do anything, how much more should we be dependent on Papa's voice? Could it be that the reason we often don't do the things that Jesus did is simply because we don't live the way He lived?

The first step to hearing God's voice is to believe that He is still speaking today. The church I grew up in taught that God no longer speaks today, and that the way He spoke in the past (through dreams, visions, angels, or His audible voice) no longer takes place because we now have the Bible to replace it. That doesn't make any sense at all either through common-sense or through theological appraisal.

Jesus said:

My sheep listen to my voice; I know them, and they follow Me. (John 10:27 NIV)

Jesus had an expectation that you would listen to His voice. How could you possibly listen to His voice if He no longer speaks today? In another verse, Job 33:14, God declares that He does speak,

...now one way, now another. (NIV)

God is still speaking today. He hasn't stopped speaking, it's just that we've forgotten how to hear Him. This guide is designed to help us remember!

Jesus had an expectation that you would listen to His voice. How could you possibly listen to His voice if He no longer speaks today?

DISCERNING THE VOICE OF THE LORD

Lesson Notes

God does speak today - I believe He's speaking constantly in many different ways. Psalm 19:1 says that the heavens declare the glory of God and the skies proclaim the work of His hands.

The problem, according to Job, is that we don't know how to hear or perceive what God is saying.

For God does speak - now one way, now another - though man may not perceive it. (Job 33:14 NIV)

In our western culture we have valued and idolized rationalism. Rationalism is defined as a belief or theory that opinions and actions should be based on reason and knowledge rather than on religious belief or emotional response. The problem with that line of thinking is that Isaiah 55:8-9 states that God's thoughts are higher than our thoughts and His ways are higher than our ways. It requires staggering amounts of pride to imagine that as Christians, our opinions and actions should be based on our human reason and human knowledge rather than on the eternal truths of God's Word!

Rationalism has led us to exalt the empirical side of life.

For example: "Show me some facts; prove it to me; I have to see it to believe it" attitude. There is nothing wrong, per se, with a desire for empirical data, but faith isn't fueled by empiricism, it is fueled by a relationship with God and a belief in His unchanging character.

It requires a staggering amount of pride to imagine that our opinions and actions should be based on our human reason and knowledge rather than on the eternal truths of God's Word!

Our school systems and churches have valued the functions of the left hemisphere of the brain: reason, logic, reading, and writing. In doing so, we have left behind valuable right hemisphere functions like imagination, creativity and intuition. These are important functions because in Numbers 12:6 the Lord declares that He reveals himself to prophets in visions and He speaks to them in dreams. Dreams and visions are more often right-brained functions.

We need to learn how God speaks rather than demand for Him to speak in the manner we choose to hear. One of the best ways to learn anything is to find an expert and do what they do. Let us apply this principle now and learn from the prophet Habakkuk.

I will stand at my watch and station myself on the ramparts; I will look to see what he will say to me, and what answer I am to give to this complaint. Then the LORD replied: "Write down the revelation and make it plain on tablets so that a herald may run with it." (Habakkuk 2:1-2 NIV)

Right now, you may be thinking, "What in the world are you talking about?" But I encourage you to stay with me. I want to break down four keys to hearing God's voice from these two small verses. Habakkuk is a prophet in the Old Testament. As you begin reading his book, it is apparent that he is lamenting to God. At the end of chapter one, the prophet asks God a series of questions, and in chapter two he prepares himself to hear God's answers.

Key #1: Quiet yourself

He says, "I will stand at my watch and station myself on the ramparts." What does that mean? He went to a place with the specific intention of hearing God speak to him and positioned himself to hear what God had to say. What this means for us is that we have to learn to quiet ourselves in the Lord's presence, which is our first key.

We need to learn how God speaks rather than demand for Him to speak in the manner we choose to hear.

Key #2: Fix your eyes on Jesus

As we read on, Habakkuk says, "I will look to see..." Habakkuk recognized the principle we talked about earlier from Numbers 12:6 - that God often speaks in vision form. A vision is simply a picture, or series of pictures (like what you see while day dreaming) that you see in your mind's eye, or with your open eye. Here we can see that he was expecting God to speak to him in a vision as he was looking to see. This is our second step; we want to look for vision while we pray. The best way to begin is to fix your eyes on Jesus (Hebrews 12:2).

Key #3: Tune to spontaneity

What happens next amuses me. It seems like a grammatical or typographical error, but the Bible records Habakkuk as saying, "I will look to see what He will say to me." Isn't that odd? You would think it should read, "I will listen to hear what He will say to me," or "I will look to see what He will show me." But be aware that God's voice often comes as a spontaneous thought. Get ready to hear God however He chooses to speak – it might come as a thought, a memory, a song, a scene from a movie, a Scripture verse that just "pops" into your head or any other creative way God chooses. If we are fixed on hearing in one specific way, we might miss what God wants to say!

Key #4: Write it down

Lastly, the prophet hears from God, and this is what the Lord says, "Write down the revelation." Do you realize that if Habakkuk hadn't obeyed that last part, we never would have known about this interaction with God? What if David hadn't penned any of his Psalms? What about John the beloved? If he hadn't written down his revelation, we'd be missing the last book of the Bible! You will want to write down what you hear or see, so that you have a copy and can share your revelations with others. This will also help you to weigh and confirm what you are hearing. (To be covered in another lesson.)

Get ready to hear God however He chooses to speak – it might come as a thought, a memory, a song... or any other creative way that God chooses.

REFLECTION AND ACTIVATION

1. Read Isaiah 6:1-7 and ask God to show you a picture of what was happening in this passage.

2. Ask Jesus what He values most about your relationship with Him. As you listen to what He says, write down what you hear.

Journal Notes

_____

_____

_____

_____

_____

_____

_____

_____

_____

_____

_____

_____

_____

_____

_____

_____

_____

_____

_____

BUT HOW DO I KNOW IT'S GOD?

Lesson Notes

Dear friends, do not believe every spirit, but test the spirits to see whether they are from God, because many false prophets have gone out into the world. (1 John 4:1 NIV)

The Apostle John wasn't kidding when he wrote these words. We want to make sure that everything we are hearing is God and not sourced in ourselves, or even worse, the enemy. So how do we know we are hearing God?

1. Confirm by Scripture

Like anything in the Christian life, we need to make sure we have a firm foundation in the teachings and doctrines of the Bible. Our first port of call is to ensure everything we are hearing lines up with the written Word of God. So the question you should always ask while reviewing your journal is, "Does what I've heard line up with the Word of God?" If it doesn't, throw it out. It doesn't matter how clearly you receive the revelation – even if an angel comes and shares something with you – none of that matters unless it coincides with Scripture. The apostle Paul spoke about this when he wrote to the Galatians.

But even if we or an angel from heaven should preach a gospel other than the one we preached to you, let him be eternally condemned!

(Galatians 1:8 NIV)

The Lord says, "Write down the revelation." You will want to write down what you hear or see.

How do you process a revelation you receive if the Scripture is silent on the issue, yet isn't necessarily contrary to? For example, if you sense the Lord instructing you to move somewhere, or He's stirring your heart toward a change of career, how can you discern and confirm the Lord's direction? There's nothing specific in Scripture directing you either way, so, what do you do?

2. Confirm by the nature of God

In these situations you may want to ask yourself, "Is what I am hearing consistent with the nature of God?" In his epistle, James writes:

But the wisdom that comes from heaven is first of all pure; then peace-loving, considerate, submissive, full of mercy and good fruit, impartial and sincere. (James 3:17 NIV)

If the revelation you receive is consistent with some of the attributes listed in that verse, it is likely that you are hearing from God.

3. Confirm by the inner witness

Even if you have a confirmation from Scripture and the nature of God supports your revelation, you also need to check your inner witness.

John wrote:

But the anointing which you have received from Him abides in you, and you do not need that anyone teach you: but as the same anointing teaches you concerning all things, and is true, and is not a lie, and just as it has taught you, you will abide in Him. (1 John 2:27 NKJV)

But the wisdom that comes from heaven is first of all pure; then peace-loving, considerate, submissive, full of mercy and good fruit, impartial and sincere. (James 3:17).

John was speaking about the witness of God that dwells within your born-again spirit. This is not a witness in your mind or even in your emotions. It is the witness in the deepest part of your being. In that place there are, what could be called, "caution lights" or "green lights." The caution light is like a little check or resistance inside your heart, even if it makes sense in your mind. The green light is a clearance within that enables you to move forward with peace, even if it doesn't make sense to the mind. The inner witness is usually extremely accurate. Remember, this is from deep within and not simply a clearance or check in the mind or emotions.

4. Confirm by fruit inspection

Finally, check the fruit of what you are hearing. For example, how does it make you feel? Are you encouraged? Uplifted? Edified? Or does the word leave you feeling condemned, guilty or fearful? The former is the "flavor" of the Holy Spirit; the latter, the enemy. Does the word you are hearing produce the fruit of the Spirit? Love, joy, peace, patience, kindness, goodness, faithfulness, gentleness and self-control are fruit the Spirit will produce when you hear His voice and act on it (according to Galatians 5:22). The fruit of the flesh is very different and includes things like selfish ambition, strife, jealousy, immorality and worldly-mindedness according to verse 19. The word you hear from the Holy Spirit will always produce good fruit.

Hearing God's thoughts are like hearing your own, with the exception that they are often light and gentle and God will typically speak in the first person. There will sometimes be unusual and surprising content – for example, the thoughts you will hear regarding the way God feels about you are probably much nicer than any thought you have ever had about yourself. God will also speak through your own personality, communication style, and vocabulary. He made you unique.

Tomorrow, we will discover another means to keep us from deception as we continue along the path to hearing God's voice more fully.

REFLECTION AND ACTIVATION

1. Read John 16:13-15. What does Jesus reveal as one of the Holy Spirit's primary jobs? How do you think the Holy Spirit does this?

2. Ask Jesus to speak to you about His plans for your relationship with Him and the Father. Ask Him what your role should be in this season.

The words you hear from the Holy Spirit will always produce good fruit.

Journal Notes

THE UMBRELLA OF PROTECTION

Lesson Notes

One of the greatest gifts you can have in life is godly leadership that cares for you. The author of Hebrews expresses this sentiment in writing:

Obey your leaders, and <u>submit</u> to them; for they watch over your soul, as those who will give an account. <u>Let them do this</u> with joy and not grief, for this would be unprofitable for you. (Hebrews 13:17)

Here we are encouraged to both obey and submit to our leaders. Neither of those terms sits well with our post-modern culture. If we have had bad examples of spiritual leaders or have been hurt in the past by authority figures we might shrink back from these commands, but this would be a tragedy. We are told to "let them do this" – the onus is on us – we choose to let them watch over our souls.

I have been blessed to have wonderful spiritual leaders – mothers and fathers in the faith who want nothing but the best for me. However, if I don't yield to the counsel and wisdom they offer or choose to submit to their direction, then I can't benefit from the very blessing God is trying to give to me through them.

It is worth noting that the Greek word used for obey in Hebrews 13:17 is *peitho* which means "to allow yourself to be persuaded by." That puts a whole new perspective on a word that perhaps we've been reluctant to use. Dr. Mark Virkler has this to say about submission:

One of the greatest gifts you can have in life is godly leadership that cares for you.

"Submission is an openness to the Spirit-led counsel and correction of several others, while keeping a sense of personal responsibility for our own discernment of God's voice within us." (p. 30, *How to Hear God's Voice*, by Mark and Patty Virkler.)

One of the reasons we have "Key 4 - Writing It Down" is that it allows us to pass our journals to those God has given us as leaders and ask for their wisdom. We submit it to them and say, "Hey... do you think this is God? What's your perspective on this?" It's another layer of safety as we grow in maturity.

To this day, I have leaders who I submit revelation to. Remember what Paul wrote in I Corinthians 13:9 – "we know in part and we prophesy in part." At best we have only one facet of the revelation God's giving us. He has put us in community to learn to trust and receive from one another.

Later in this study we will talk more about what kind of leaders you desire to be submitted to, but for now let's define the search engine as this: Leaders whose lives and fruit are in keeping with a deep understanding of God's love for His children. Leaders who are constantly in pursuit of healing and wholeness in their own lives and demonstrate a genuine and life-giving relationship with the Trinity. People whose lives are not all about themselves but are focused on the needs, desires, and dreams of others are able to encourage you while guarding against error. They can dream with you while providing wisdom. Leaders who demonstrate a desire for their ceiling to be your floor and will open doors for you to succeed.

REFLECTION AND ACTIVATION

1. Read 2 Corinthians 13:1b. Why do you think it's wiser to submit your journal to more than one person? Ask the Father to show you who could help you grow as you are learning to journal. Who could you trust with your journal? Ask the Father to share how much He loves you.

Submission is an openness to the Spirit-led counsel of others, while keeping a sense of personal responsibility for our own discernment of God's voice.

Journal Notes

YOUR FOCUS IS IMPORTANT

Lesson Notes

This is what the Sovereign LORD says: When any Israelite sets up idols in his heart and puts a wicked stumbling block before his face and then goes to a prophet, I the LORD will answer him myself in keeping with his great idolatry. (Ezekiel 14:4 NIV)

Have you ever asked God about a situation in prayer but were more concerned with hearing the answer you wanted to hear instead of the one He wanted to give? Often with large purchases, things we covet after, or romantic relationships, we so desperately want to "hear God" say, "YES!" Only afterwards we realize we only listened for what we wanted to hear.

This principle is called "listening through an idol" and is what today's Bible verse refers to. When we create a place in our heart for an idol (the thing we want more than God's revelation on the topic), and then go to God for revelation, our heart isn't actually postured to receive God's wisdom.

The issue is where we place our focus. If we fix our eyes on Jesus and only want His will and His answer, He will answer according to that posture. If, however, we want our own way and are focused on our idol, (whatever that may be), often we have already determined in our heart that we will do what we want regardless and we simply want to hear

If we fix our eyes on Jesus and only want His will and His answer, He will answer according to that posture.

"Go on my child," to pacify what we know is wrong. According to the book of Ezekiel, the Lord will answer us according to our idolatry. That's a scary thought!

This was Balaam's problem. You can read all about Balaam and his famous donkey in Numbers 22, but the executive summary goes something like this: Balaam is hired by Balak to put a curse on God's chosen people. Balaam is very wise – before doing anything he asks the Lord what to do and the Lord says, "Do not go... You must not put a curse on those people, because they are blessed" (Numbers 22:12). Balaam then delivers the news and refuses to go with them.

However we read a very interesting phrase in verses 15-17:

Then Balak sent other princes, more numerous and more distinguished than the first... they came... and said... "I will reward you handsomely and do whatever you say. Come and put a curse on these people for me." (NIV)

Despite already knowing the heart of God in this matter, Balaam is recorded as asking the Lord if he can go a second time. What's staggering is that verse 20 says that God came to Balaam and said "go with them." However, the following verse reveals what's actually occurring:

Balaam got up in the morning, saddled his donkey and went with the princes of Moab. But God was very angry when he went... (NIV)

Why was God angry with him for going, when verse 20 says that God said to go with them? What's going on here? It's the principle from Ezekiel 14 in action - Balaam was listening through an idol. Despite having heard clearly from God, his heart was swayed by the distinguished princes and the handsome rewards. God answered him according to what he wanted to hear. Balaam knew the will of God as a result of hearing His word the first time he sought Him. Unfortunately, the second time, he approached him "through his idols."

The good news, however, is that we are now aware of this principle and can avoid being tripped up by the enemy. Let's get rid of our idols and seek the Lord's ways and not our own!

The good news is that we can avoid being tripped up by the enemy. Let us seek the Lord's ways and not our own!

REFLECTION AND ACTIVATION

1. Read 2 Peter 2:15. What was the sin of Balaam that Peter is talking about here? How can you avoid the same errors?

2. Can you identify a time when you had an idol in your heart?

3. Journal and ask the Lord any question you wish, so long as it is not the most pressing issue in in your life right now.

Journal Notes

_____

_____

_____

_____

_____

_____

_____

_____

_____

_____

_____

_____

_____

_____

_____

_____

_____

_____

_____

DEVELOPING A LIFESTYLE OF LISTENING TO GOD

Lesson Notes

But solid food is for the mature, who by constant use have trained themselves to distinguish good from evil. (Hebrews 5:14 NIV)

If you were to ask someone who was skilled in a certain area how they became so proficient, more often than not their answer would be "I practiced." That is true, also, in the realms of the spirit. The writer of Hebrews alludes to this principle in the verse above. The mature became mature by constant use of their disciplines and gifts and as a result, they trained themselves to distinguish good from evil.

I have been following the four keys (taught in Lesson Notes for Week One-Day One), for over eight years now. For many of those years I journaled daily. That constant practice honed my senses and refined my spirit to discern what is of God and what is not of Him. I find it much easier now to clearly discern the voice of God than when I first started.

My encouragement to you is to make journaling part of your lifestyle and your devotional life with God. I have found that journaling works best when used in the context of relationship rather than for accessing revelation. By that I mean, 90% of my journaling is for my edification, for my comfort, and for my personal growth. Only 10% of the time does God give me external revelation. If you focus on the wrong thing and only come to God when needing something, you've missed the point. God is hungry for your time, He desires your company, and He wants

God is hungry for your time, He desires your company, and He wants to speak to you.

to speak to you. He is not interested in merely telling you "stuff," but rather in sharing His heart and hearing yours.

As you head into this wonderful journey of discovering God's Fathering heart for you, take time to ask Him questions, to seek His heart and to enter His presence. Enjoy the journey!

REFLECTION AND ACTIVATION

1. Read Luke 5:16 and Exodus 33:7-9.
    What similarities do you see here? Why the need for solitude? How can you emulate the same principle in your life?

2. Ask the Father to reveal a practical time that you can meet with Him in this season of your life. Set that time aside and practice journaling in His presence.

Journal Notes

_____

_____

_____

_____

_____

_____

_____

_____

_____

_____

_____

_____

_____

_____

_____

SOAKING

Be still, and know that I am God; I will be exalted among the nations, I will be exalted in the earth. (Psalm 46:10 NIV)

Many Christians want to know God and encounter a deeper relationship with Him. They want to see His glory among the nations and desire to see Him exalted in the earth, but they forget the first part of this verse - to be still. In forgetting this, they turn to what we, as a human race are very good at: striving. However, striving only leads to frustration. This principle of stillness and rest is found elsewhere in Scripture:

This is what the Sovereign LORD, the Holy One of Israel, says: "In repentance and rest is your salvation, in quietness and trust is your strength, but you would have none of it." (Isaiah 30:15 NIV)

Waiting on the Lord and resting in His Presence gives you strength.

Our salvation is found through repentance and *rest*. Typically we are very good at the former and terrible at the latter. The Lord also says that strength is found in quietness and trust. Most Christians I've met are constantly moving with a frantic nervous energy, and in the midst of it, they are trying to trust and find God. It's not meant to be like that. The key to your walk with God is resting in Him. It's about spending time in His Presence.

Even youths will become exhausted, and young men will give up. But those who wait on the LORD will find new strength. They will fly high on wings like eagles. They will run and not grow weary. They will walk and not faint. (Isaiah 40:30-31 NLT)

Waiting on the Lord and resting in His Presence gives you strength. What does that actually look like? How do you do that? Well, that's the beautiful thing - you have to do very little. In fact, if you do it right, you do nothing! Intrigued? Read on.

CHOOSING THE BETTER PART

Lesson Notes

As Jesus and His disciples were on their way, He came to a village where a woman named Martha opened her home to Him. She had a sister called Mary, who sat at the Lord's feet listening to what He said. But Martha was distracted by all the preparations that had to be made. She came to Him and asked, "Lord, don't you care that my sister has left me to do the work by myself? Tell her to help me!"

"Martha, Martha," the Lord answered, "you are worried and upset about many things, but only one thing is needed. Mary has chosen what is better, and it will not be taken away from her." (Luke 10:38-42 NIV)

Mary sat at the Lord's feet and listened to what He said. She chose to be near the Lord in the midst of busyness.

In our walk with God there will always be work to do; there will always be preparations that need to be made - but the smartest thing to do is to choose the better part. In Luke's account above, we see that Mary sat at the Lord's feet and listened to what He said. She chose to be near the Lord in the midst of busyness. One of the disciplines we need to cultivate is that of drawing near to God. James said it well:

Draw close to God, and God will draw close to you. (James 4:8 NLT)

When we choose to draw close to God, He chooses to draw close to us. It's as simple as that.

In Moses' day, we read that he pitched the tent of meeting outside the camp of the Israelites (Exodus 33:7). He moved away from his daily responsibilities by physically going to a different place and there he met with the Lord. During those times the Lord met with Moses face to face as a friend meets with a friend. I can't imagine how busy Moses was as he led the Israelites through the wilderness - but in the midst of his busy schedule he made time to seek the Lord and spend time with Him.

REFLECTION AND ACTIVATION

1. Do you think if Moses hadn't gone to be with the Lord in the tent of meeting the Lord would have come to him?

2. Find a time today to be still - set aside at least 30 minutes - get a pillow for your head, and some quiet music to rest to. Lie down and simply pray this, "Come Holy Spirit" and then wait upon the Lord.

Journal Notes

_____

_____

_____

_____

_____

_____

_____

_____

_____

_____

_____

_____

_____

_____

_____

_____

_____

SOUL RESTORATION

Lesson Notes

The LORD is my shepherd, I shall not be in want. He makes me lie down in green pastures, He leads me beside quiet waters, He restores my soul. He guides me in paths of righteousness for His name's sake. Even though I walk through the valley of the shadow of death, I will fear no evil, for You are with me; Your rod and your staff, they comfort me. You prepare a table before me in the presence of my enemies. You anoint my head with oil; my cup overflows. Surely goodness and love will follow me all the days of my life, and I will dwell in the house of the LORD forever.

(Psalm 23 NIV)

God wants to restore your soul. Having saved it, He wants to keep you refreshed, renewed and restored. He wants to guide you in paths of righteousness. Often in the busyness of life, we forget these things. In the midst of turmoil and day-to-day living we can forget that God wants to comfort us and prepare a place of victory for us. I have found that when I choose to rest in God my soul gets restored. My hope and my excitement in God get renewed and I experience His love and His affection. I begin to encounter goodness and love in a tangible way.

My journey into soaking was a difficult one. I found the thought of lying down and doing nothing offensive, as I couldn't see how that would accomplish anything. As someone with a type A personality, I would find it hard to quiet my mind as I was constantly thinking about things to do, things I forgot to accomplish that day, phone calls I needed

In the midst of turmoil and day-to-day living we can forget that God wants to comfort us and prepare a place of victory for us.

to make, etc. But with practice I got good at quieting myself down, fixing my eyes on Jesus, and resting in His presence. And what a difference it made! I would say that soaking - resting in his presence - has made the biggest difference in my personal walk with God.

Reading about soaking is one thing, but doing it is something altogether different!

REFLECTION AND ACTIVATION

1. Using last week's teaching on journaling, ask the Lord what He wants to accomplish through soaking with you.

2. Lie down, welcome the Holy Spirit, and play some soft music. Soak for 30 minutes; don't pray, don't speak in tongues, don't strive - just rest in His presence and experience His love.

Journal Notes

_____

_____

_____

_____

_____

_____

_____

_____

_____

_____

_____

_____

_____

_____

_____

_____

_____

_____

FINDING FATHER 43

REMAIN IN THE VINE

Jesus gives us the key to fruitfulness in life – which is intimacy with Him.

Lesson Notes

Remain in me, and I will remain in you. No branch can bear fruit by itself; it must remain in the vine. Neither can you bear fruit unless you remain in me. I am the vine; you are the branches. If a man remains in me and I in him, he will bear much fruit; apart from me you can do nothing.

(John 15:4-5 NIV)

In today's passage, Jesus gives us the key to fruitfulness in life – which is intimacy with Him. We are to cultivate a friendship with God by spending time with Him, just like Jesus did when He was here on earth. (Luke 5:16)

I have spent many, many hours soaking in His presence listening for His voice and resting in His love. After soaking, I love to journal so I have record of my special time with Him. Soaking and journaling have transformed my life, ministry, and relationship with God.

Many years ago my husband Alyn travelled to attend a conference where John & Carol Arnott from Toronto were ministering. He knew of their ministry and the revival that started at their church. They had wonderfully stewarded this move of God for many years and he wanted to learn from them both. Alyn attended a workshop featuring Carol called, "The Key to Personal Revival." He thought to himself, "Yes! This is what I've come for! I am going to get the keys to revival and power!" Imagine his shock and horror when Carol began to teach on intimacy and divine romance! Here he was, a 27 year-old single guy and she was talking about mushy stuff! Where was the power? Where was the revival? Where were the glory clouds? Intimacy and divine romance was not what he thought had he signed up for!

But then he had an inner thought rise up in him that sounded like this, "They've been in revival for years and they carry the glory of God with them – you don't. Perhaps you should do what they do and you'll get what they've got." Well, that sounded like Wisdom to him! So he listened attentively as Carol taught all about soaking and resting in God's Presence.

When he returned from the conference, he took one month off from his normal devotional life that consisted only of Bible study and prayer. He decided to soak for one month instead. At the beginning it was very difficult for him. It felt like a waste of time. It felt like he wasn't doing anything! His "doer" was dying within him. However, by the end of the month things had changed and he was experiencing the presence of God in new and very tangible ways. In short, God was showing up and Alyn was "remaining" in Him. He was soaking in Him. He was receiving Father's heart.

Rest and soak in His presence. Ask for His tangible presence to fill your room as you rest in Him.

REFLECTION AND ACTIVATION

1. Read John 15:9-10. How did the Father love Jesus? With that in mind, how does Jesus love you? What two things does Jesus ask us to do in life according to this passage?

2. Grab a pillow, a soaking CD and lie down to rest and soak in His presence. Ask for His tangible presence to fill your room as you rest in Him.

Journal Notes

REST IS GOD'S AGENDA FOR YOU

Lesson Notes

Waiting on the Lord and resting in His presence gives you strength to move on in life.

Come to Me, all you who are weary and burdened, and I will give you rest. Take My yoke upon you and learn from Me, for I am gentle and humble in heart, and you will find rest for your souls. For My yoke is easy and My burden is light. (Matthew 11:28-30 NIV)

In this verse Jesus makes several promises. First, if we come to Him, He will give us rest. Secondly, if we take His yoke upon us (i.e. His agenda for our lives) and learn from Him, we will find rest for our souls. It's interesting that the result of both of these promises is rest. Not power, not authority, not glory, not mission statements, not destiny - but rest. One of the Lord's primary agendas for your life is that you would be a person of rest. Rest is a weapon that the Lord will use powerfully against the enemy who opposes you.

This is the same principle that we looked at on Day 1 this week.

Even youths will become exhausted, and young men will give up. But those who wait on the LORD will find new strength. They will fly high on wings like eagles. They will run and not grow weary. They will walk and not faint. (Isaiah 40:30-31 NLT)

Waiting on the Lord and resting in His presence gives you strength to move on in life. If you are finding yourself doing things because of stress, or duty, or perceived responsibility, it is possible you could be headed for burn out. Rather, we are to move out of rest; out of a re-focused life. Heidi Baker - one of the busiest people I know - says this, "All fruitfulness flows out of intimacy with God." In taking time to rest we become a people of confidence, of resolution, of vision and of authority.

Moses found this out when he was asking the Lord to help him lead God's people. One of the requests Moses made was to know God better (Exodus 33:13).

What was the Lord's response?

The LORD replied, "My Presence will go with you, and I will give you rest."

(Exodus 33:14 NIV)

Get into the Lord's Presence and you will find rest.

REFLECTION AND ACTIVATION

1. Ask the Lord why rest is high on His agenda? Invite Him to show you how to find rest in the midst of your life.

2. Enter God's rest today (Hebrews 4:11) through soaking in His presence. Try soaking for 40 minutes today and pay attention to what you feel as you rest.

One of the Lord's primary agendas for your life is that you would be a person of rest.

Journal Notes

DEVELOPING A LIFESTYLE OF INTIMACY

Lesson Notes

Rest is a weapon that the Lord will use powerfully against the enemy who opposes you.

Enoch walked with God; then he was no more, because God took him away. (Genesis 5:24 NIV)

One of my most favorite characters in the Bible is Enoch. Not much is written about Enoch but we know this about him: he walked with God and then God took him away. The writer of Hebrews adds this information:

By faith Enoch was taken from this life, so that he did not experience death; he could not be found, because God had taken him away. For before he was taken, he was commended as one who pleased God.

(Hebrews 11:5 NIV)

The phrase "walked with God" is an interesting one. It's sparingly attributed elsewhere in Scripture, but perhaps the description of Noah's life gives us a glimpse of what it really means:

This is the account of Noah. Noah was a righteous man, blameless among the people of his time, and he walked with God.

(Genesis 6:9 NIV)

It suggests a lifetime of intimacy, relationship, obedience, and friendship. I think Enoch walked with God so closely that God couldn't stand to have a physical separation, so He took him up to heaven to be with Him. As far as we know, he is probably still up there!

You see, God is so in love with us, and so delighted with us, that He wants to cultivate a friendship so deep and rich that He can't bear to be separated from us. That's the reason Jesus came of course; to restore relationship with the Father so that we could be one again. This intimacy isn't something that's reserved for some far off distant date when we die and are with Him – it's something that can be enjoyed now, here on earth.

Alyn and I have a dear friend named Adele. One day Adele was sharing with us her perspectives on soaking. She said, "Jesus says, 'Ask and you will receive.' So, how is it that we're very good at the asking part but not so good with the 'receiving' part?'" Adele went on to explain that if we are the ones doing all the talking, our conversation is one-sided. Soaking is the listening part of our conversation with Him. Soaking is setting aside time to lie down and receive from Him. Soaking is to REST IN HIS LOVE as opposed to STRIVING IN PRAYER.

I want to suggest to you that soaking is one of the most helpful things you will find in cultivating a lifestyle of intimacy with God.

REFLECTION AND ACTIVATION

1. Today, set aside an hour to be with God. Put on your favorite CD and rest in His presence. Ask Him to come and reveal His love for you. As you marinate in His presence, thank Him for His goodness, kindness and faithfulness.

The reason Jesus came was to restore relationship with the Father so that we could be one again.

Journal Notes

INTRODUCTION TO THE FATHER'S HEART

In 1991, a friend of mine hijacked me and brought me to a little church at the end of an airport runway in Toronto. At the time I was in really rough shape. I was struggling with suicidal thoughts almost 24 hours a day, and I was slowly losing my grip on reality. I had just finished writing some letters to my family about why I was going to end my life. In this condition, my friend Sandi and I walked into the back of this little church. To be honest, I didn't want to be there, and I was not happy with Sandi for bringing me there either. We normally attended another church on Sundays where I had been plotting my own demise in the second row while people seemed to be completely oblivious to the pain I was in. So, one sunny Sunday morning, Sandi decided to take us to a different church. I had no idea how much it would change my life.

I remember the day very well... the worship pastor began to sing a song called, "Father I Want You to Hold Me," and I began to unravel.

I remember the day very well, actually. We sat two rows from the back even though there was plenty of room up front. As the worship started, Jeremy Sinnott (the worship pastor) began to sing a song called, "Father I Want You to Hold Me," and I began to unravel. You see, my own dad had killed himself just months before and that had led to my downward spiral. I was a professional at putting on a good face. I doubt even Sandi knew how desperate things had become for me. The truth is, I was on the edge of just not making it. So here I was in a new church practically against my will, where instead of singing "happy, clappy, songs," Jeremy and the team were going right for the heart; and I lost it. I mean, completely lost it! There I was a few rows from the back sobbing and wailing through the entire music set.

Try as I might I could not stop the tears, sobbing and shaking. When worship was over, we all sat down and I proceeded to cry all the way through the message. I mean, this might be normal behavior for some people, but not for me. I didn't cry in public *ever*. In fact, I often mocked others who did! You know, those people who cry at the sappy part in a movie or while watching TV. Oh yes, I mocked them with glee!

When John Arnott finished speaking (I still don't know what he spoke on that day because I couldn't hear him over the noise I was making), he looked around with those kind eyes and said, "There is someone here who needs to know that Daddy loves them." Could that have been for me? I remember thinking, "I am *so* not going up there! There are 60 people here watching me!" But apparently my body had plans of its own, or so it seemed - I found myself walking up to the front of the church before my brain could have its say. As I approached the front, John simply opened up his arms. I walked into them and cried all over him for about 40 minutes. And, oh, I mean the full deal here: snot, tears, the whole gamut! At times I am pretty sure John was holding me up as God began to wash over me. Through the tears and deep cries, the pain in my heart found a voice and release.

When I was finally able to pull myself together, John introduced me to Jeremy (the worship leader) and a man named Ian Ross who was another father-figure in the church. What started for me that day was a one-and-a-half year season where every Sunday one of these three men would meet with me. Even if it was only for a few minutes, they would encourage me, pray for me, and give me a hug. God used their arms to begin to love me back to life. I wish I could say all of my issues melted away on that first day, but the truth is they didn't. There were plenty of issues to work through; however, when you know God's Fathering heart personally, you can tackle any mountains - even ones in the past.

So, a year-and-a-half down the road you might think I was really together and fully knew Papa God's heart for me, but honestly, I still didn't get it! Every Sunday morning at Toronto Airport Christian Fellowship somehow, the message of the Father's heart and His love for us would be woven into the sermon and I would just get frustrated! Yes! Yes, we know He loves us. MOVE ON!!! Well, I suppose they didn't move on because there is nothing to move on to. God is Love. Still, there I was getting frustrated at having to hear it again. (Side note: When we are frustrated by the message of Father's love toward us, that's a pretty good indication that we still don't really get it!) At that point, I could tell you all the verses

When you know God's Fathering heart personally, you can tackle any mountains.

and explain to you how we know we are loved, but I didn't live like I was loved. I was frustrated by the topic and numb to it all. So, a year and a half later, on one particular Sunday morning, a minister began to speak and I remember saying to God, "God why do we have to hear the message again?" He answered me, "Because Sweetheart, you still don't get it." As you might imagine I cried a bit that morning, and then I decided to surrender to Papa God my plans and what I thought I needed to hear and understand. I chose to submit to His plans and what He knew I actually needed. He knew I needed the message of His acceptance and unconditional love for me. He knew I wasn't really receiving the message in my heart. I was so occupied running to busyness and hyper-religious activity to dull that pain. Yet, all the while, God knew I actually needed to rest in His love and let Him heal me.

That Sunday night before I went to bed I prayed a simple prayer that went something like this: "Father, I know I don't understand this message of Your love for me. I don't know what is in the way, but my heart's desire is to get what all the fuss is about! Please help me get it."

That night I had a dream. I had the exact same dream seven times over the next two years, and God used this dream to awaken my heart. It was a dream about the Father's house and while the dream would take too long to tell, the end is what is important. In the dream I am standing in the Father's bedroom and there is a large bed at least twice my height in front of me. I am jumping to try and reach the top of the mattress but there is just no way. I know the Father is up there on the bed and I can vaguely see him through the veil surrounding this massive structure. Suddenly, the curtains open on the window, the sun shines in the room, and I am lifted through the air past the veil and into the Father's lap! He holds me and we start laughing together and then I wake up.

As I woke up from the first time I had the dream, I could hear God audibly laughing in my bedroom for about 10 seconds. It was an incredible sound so full of love and joy as to make you cry with it. After lying in bed savoring the sound of God's laughter I heard a verse go through my head that I had never understood before… and that's where the journey began.

God knew I actually needed to rest in His love and let Him heal me.

THE WAY HOME

Lesson Notes

The first verse that echoed through my consciousness was one I had heard a million times before – but there was something very important that I had missed. Let's look at it and perhaps you will understand what I mean…

Jesus said… "I am the way, and the truth, and the life."

Jesus said to him, "I am the way, and the truth, and the life; no one comes to the Father but through Me." (John 14:6)

You have most likely heard this verse many times before. I had always heard it used in evangelism messages. But here is what God asked me that morning: "The way to whom?" I was dumbfounded! What do you mean, God? Here is the thing I missed… for Jesus to be "The Way" there must be a destination! He is the way to what? To Whom? Jesus is the way to the Father.

Let's look for just a moment at why Jesus came. It is pretty clear from looking at John 3:16 -17, it was a relationship rescue mission.

For (Father) God so loved the world, that He gave His only begotten Son, that whoever believes in Him shall not perish, but have eternal life. For (Father) God did not send the Son into the world to judge the world, but that the world might be saved through Him.

(John 3:16-17 NASB - Amplification mine)

I don't know about you, but I had so many wrong ideas about why Jesus came. From this passage we see the reason very clearly – it was love. In the Greek, that word "love" in this passage is the word Agape, which means unconditional love; the unconditional love of a Father for his children. Only that depth of love could motivate that kind of sacrifice we witness in the Father asking His only Son to go to the cross. Jesus didn't come to judge us or give us a set of rules to live by; He came to restore relationship with the Father. He came to make a "way" home for us and yet, still so many of us get lost along the way.

REFLECTION AND ACTIVATION

1. Spend some time soaking in the Father's Presence. Invite Him to come really close and reveal His Father's heart toward you. Now rest and let Him wash over you. If you have had a hard time "getting to" the Father, when you lay down to soak, start by asking Jesus to come and be "The Way" and help you reach the Father.

2. After soaking, grab your journal and ask Father a few questions. Using the teaching from Week 1 on Hearing God's Voice, start by asking…

3. Daddy God, what do you want my heart to know today?

Jesus came to restore relationship with the Father. He came to make a "way" home for us.

Journal Notes

JESUS AND THE FATHER ARE EXACTLY THE SAME

Lesson Notes

So how is it that we get so confused about what Father God is like and how He sees us? In a word - LIFE. Our experiences in life condition us to respond to the world around us and to God. For example, some of us grew up with the idea of God as a big policeman in the sky just waiting for us to make a mistake so He could pounce on us. With that type of outlook, it's no wonder that we would have some wrong views of Father God! As we are spending the entire fourth week talking about our wrong views of God and dismantling them, let's lay down some groundwork from Scripture.

Because I didn't have a great view of Father God, I had only ever related to Jesus or the Holy Spirit. In fact, I imagined that when I needed something or did something wrong, Jesus was standing between myself and an angry God, pleading for mercy that was barely granted! This couldn't be less true. Let's look at this verse from John 16…

God wants us to experience His love and we do not need to fear, bribe, whine, strive, or contrive in requesting anything from the Father because He loves us!

> *In that day you will ask in My name, and I do not say to you that I will request of the Father on your behalf; for the Father Himself loves you.*
>
> *(John 16:26-27)*

The word "love" in this passage is the Greek word Phileo; which means experiential love. God wants us to experience His love and we do not need to fear, bribe, whine, strive, or contrive in requesting anything from the Father because He loves us!

Let's look at another verse in the book of Hebrews:

And He is the radiance of His glory and the exact representation of His nature…. (Hebrews 1:3a)

I love this verse in The Message translation as well…..

This Son perfectly mirrors God, and is stamped with God's nature.

Jesus is the exact representation of the Father. So, what we know about Jesus we know about Father God, as well! What do we know about Jesus, then? Take a minute right now and write down a few things we know about Him from Scripture…

_____

_____

_____

_____

_____

_____

Jesus is the exact representation of the Father. So, what we know about Jesus we know about Father God, as well!

This is what I came up with when God asked me to write a list many years ago: He loves me, He loves children, He is my friend, He intercedes for me, He is my savior, He is my healer, He laughs, He cries, He cares how I am doing…

Do you realize that Scripture says Jesus only did what He saw the Father doing, and He only said what He heard the Father saying?

Jesus answered: "Don't you know me, Philip, even after I have been among you such a long time? Anyone who has seen Me has seen the Father. How can you say, 'Show us the Father'?' Don't you believe that I am in the Father, and that the Father is in Me? The words I say to you are not just my own. Rather, it is the Father, living in Me, who is doing his work." (John 14:9-10 NIV)

If Jesus is the exact representation of the Father, then all of those things and more are true of Papa God also! You see, at some point we have to come to the realization that either our own perception of God is right and that He is distant, angry and uncaring (or whatever belief you had about Him), or Scripture is right and our perception is wrong! I know I wasn't going to be the first person on earth to prove God wrong, so I asked God to reveal to me each place in my life where I had misjudged His heart toward me as a Father.

REFLECTION AND ACTIVATION

1. Grab your soaking CD and a pillow and hit the floor. Again, ask the Father to reveal new things about Himself to you today while you rest in His Presence.

2. After soaking, grab your journal and spend some time asking Papa a few questions like:

3. In what ways do I still see Jesus as the One who protects me from Your hand?

At some point we have to come to the realization that either our own perception of God is right and that He is distant, angry and uncaring, or Scripture is right and our perception is wrong!

Journal Notes

SIGNIFICANCE

Lesson Notes

One of the definitions of a "Father" in the dictionary is: "The person we get our significance from." So what happens if our own fathers were not healed enough to speak significance into us? Or, what if your Dad left when you were young, or you have never met him? Or what if he simply was not able to speak significance and healing into you because it was never shown to him? As a result of these types of scenarios, many of us could easily wander through life never able to relate to a God that would take any interest in us. Why would a God we can't see or touch take an interest in us when our own fathers didn't? Oh, but He does!

The truth is, God is so interested in you that Scripture says He numbered the very hairs on your head! For some of us thick-haired folks that took a lot of time! You are so significant that He would have sent Jesus to die on the cross just for you. You are so significant that He took the time to weave you together in your mother's womb. He picked your hair color, the color of your eyes, how tall you would be, the shape of your nose... everything! That's significant!

Definition of Significance

significance | sig-nifikəns | | s-g-n-f1kəns | | s-g-n-f-k(ə)ns |

noun

1) the quality of being worthy of attention; importance

You are so significant that He would have sent Jesus to die on the cross just for you. You are so significant that He took the time to weave you together in your mother's womb.

Look at this passage from Psalm 139 …

For You formed my inward parts; You wove me in my mother's womb. I will give thanks to You, for I am fearfully and wonderfully made; Wonderful are Your works, And my soul knows it very well. My frame was not hidden from You, When I was made in secret, And skillfully wrought in the depths of the earth; Your eyes have seen my unformed substance; And in Your book were all written the days that were ordained for me, When as yet there was not one of them. (Psalm 139:13-16)

You are not a mistake or even a surprise! You may have been a surprise to your parents, but you were never a surprise to Father. He made you and He says you are fearfully and wonderfully made! God doesn't make any mistakes and He made you as you are, and He calls you by name as His Child. You are incredibly significant!

REFLECTION AND ACTIVATION

1. Ask Holy Spirit to reveal any areas of your life where you doubted your significance to your Heavenly Father. Journal the thoughts the Spirit reveals to you. Ask Father what He wants to say about those things. Wait for Him to speak. Journal the things He speaks to your heart.

2. Ask Holy Spirit to reveal to you the areas of your life where you believe you are unworthy of Father's attention. Journal the thoughts the Spirit reveals to you.

3. Ask Father what He wants to say about those things. Wait for Him to speak. Journal the things He speaks to your heart.

4. When you have completed journaling about this topic, grab your pillow and your soaking music and lay down again. Invite Papa to speak His significance into you.

You were never a surprise to Father. He made you and He says you are fearfully and wonderfully made!

Journal Notes

IT'S A PROCESS, FOLKS…

Believing is different from knowing in the sense that knowing comes from the head and believing comes from the heart.

Lesson Notes

A few days after I had the dream I previously mentioned, I stumbled across a verse that gave me great hope!

We have come to know and have believed the love which God has for us. God is love, and the one who abides in love abides in God, and God abides in him. (1John 4:16)

Today, let's look at the first part of that verse. It says, "We have come to know." That word "know" in the Greek is the word "ginosko" and it refers to a mental recognition of a truth. So, at some point our brains will come on board with the truth that we are loved. But that's not all; it then says, "and have believed." That word believed is the word "pisteuo" in the Greek that means to entrust or put faith in. It is our hearts that have faith and are able to trust even when our heads are still skeptical. Believing is different from knowing in the sense that knowing comes from the head and believing comes from the heart.

Have you noticed that God usually imparts information and insight to your brain first where you can begin to chew on it and think it through? That is a good process but ultimately, it needs to move to your heart where it can be pumped into the very fiber of your being. You see, it's only when that information takes up residence in your heart and becomes revelation that you will begin to live like it is true!

We have come to know and have believed the love which God has for us. (1 John 4:16)

What are we knowing and believing in again? "The love which God has for us." The word "love" in this verse is the word "agape" in the Greek. Agape is the unconditional love of God.

We will talk more about unconditional love tomorrow, but for now we can rest in the fact that we are in process! Not one of us has arrived yet, but God is working on each of us to move our head knowledge to heart knowledge.

How do we know when we are making progress? When we wake up and walk around everyday knowing deep inside that we are fully loved and accepted. Our insecurities melt away in the face of such love. We have no fear for what the future holds because we are loved by the most wonderful Father who has incredible plans to bless us and not to harm us. We are able to love others instead of compete with them because we know we are special to Him – significant and chosen. When we start to respond in this fashion to our day and the people in it, you can bet there has been some serious movement from the head down that 12 – 18 inches (depending on our height of course) to our hearts. We live like we are loved.

We have no fear for what the future holds because we are loved by the most wonderful Father who has incredible plans to bless us and not to harm us.

REFLECTION AND ACTIVATION

Let's journal first again today.

1. Ask the Father what head knowledge He wants to move to your heart today. Journal what He speaks to your heart. Then grab your pillow and get ready to soak in His love.

Journal Notes

_____

_____

_____

_____

_____

_____

_____

_____

_____

_____

_____

_____

_____

_____

_____

_____

_____

_____

_____

_____

_____

_____

_____

_____

AGAPE

Lesson Notes

The word agape is one of four Greek words that we translate to the English word, "love." The Greeks recognized different kinds of love and named each one of them accordingly. When we read through Scripture, it's often helpful to be able to check what the original text says when we read words like "love." We are going to look at the Greek word "agape" today. Remember, agape, as previously stated means unconditional love or selfless love.

God loves us despite our challenges of heart, and He loves us past our moments when the rest of the world might turn their backs on us.

Here are some familiar agape verses:

For God so loved the world, that He gave His only begotten Son, that whoever believes in Him shall not perish, but have eternal life. (John 3:16)

And hope does not disappoint, because the love of God has been poured out within our hearts through the Holy Spirit who was given to us. (Romans 5:5)

But God demonstrates His own love toward us, in that while we were yet sinners, Christ died for us. (Romans 5:8)

Most of us don't know what to do with the concept of being loved without condition. Even if we are incredibly healed individuals, it's difficult to love unconditionally. Even with those closest to us we may have negative reaction moments such as: "Why on earth would you have done such and such? What were you thinking?" Or, "I am not sure I want to be with you right now!"

Unconditional love is tricky for us but not for God. He doesn't love us only when we are perfect people or when we always get it right. If that were the case, there would be no one left to love. He loves us despite our challenges of heart, and He loves us past our moments when the rest of the world might turn their backs on us. Papa doesn't know how to love us halfway. John Arnott pastored me for many years and would constantly say, "God loves you just the way you are but he loves you too much to leave you that way." That truth brings peace to my heart in the present moment of stress when I am reminded that because of Father's goodness, "It's going to be OK … I am loved." It also brings hope for the future that I am a work-in-progress and He really will see me through to completion (Philippians 1:6).

REFLECTION AND ACTIVATION

1. Invite Holy Spirit to help you answer the following questions and journal the answers: What areas of your life are you trying to make perfect so you can be loved by God?

2. In what areas of your past are you uncomfortable with the idea of unconditional love?

3. In what moments of your life has God tried to show you His unconditional love?

Yep, you guessed it: It's soaking time! You may want to take a few moments at the beginning to forgive yourself for any of those things that God has brought up while you were journaling, especially anything you are still holding yourself hostage for.

Now grab your pillow, get comfortable and let Him wash you clean of all those past mistakes and shame that He wants to lift off your heart.

God loves you just the way you are but He loves you too much to leave you that way.

Journal Notes

HINDRANCES

This week we are going to look at some of the hindrances to being able to enter God's Presence and experience His unconditional love. The process of identifying and removing stumbling blocks has no doubt already begun for you and will likely continue, but this week we want to look at some of the main hindrances that seem to be present in most individuals.

Some of these hindrances are simply the result of conditioning. We go through life and learn methods of coping and behaving and then carry those ways on into our new life with God.

Put another way, it seems that when we get saved we bring all of our previous issues to church with us. There is no doubt that God deals with many things right away, but if we give way to the mindsets and behaviors of our old man it can affect our relationships with God and others. The way that we have lived for many years in our everyday life has become so normal to us that it can determine how we function at church and relate to God.

God wants us to experience Him! The Word says to "taste and see that the Lord is good." But when we have these walls in place between God and us, we end up frustrated and alone.

Now, I am sure none of us are running around thinking, "Thank you, but I shall keep my hindrances as they are now my friends." However, we can certainly be in the place where we believe that our way of thinking and behaving is normal; or even what God wants us to be like. This can actually keep us locked in to some of these cycles!

God wants us to experience Him! The Word says to "taste and see that the Lord is good." But when we have these walls in place between God and us, we end up frustrated and alone. We might even think that God does not desire to be close to us. Well, that just isn't the case! He is all about relationship and you are His beloved child. He longs to love on you, to call you to life, and to share each day with Him. We need to remove the hindrances that stop us from having the kind of relationship that He desires us to have with Him.

THE HINDRANCE OF FEAR

Lesson Notes

Many of us have an unhealthy fear of God and then wonder why we feel so distant from Him. Our walls of fear are keeping Him out.

Our first hindrance that we are going to look at is fear. Let's face it, no one wants to be in relationship with someone they are afraid of. I am sure there is not one of us that walks into a party and looks for the scariest, mean-faced individual to strike up a conversation with and befriend. Of course not! We choose those who we would be able to trust. But many of us have an unhealthy fear of God and then wonder why we feel so distant from Him. Our walls of fear are keeping Him out. There may be very understandable reasons for those walls to be there, such as a difficult childhood or abuse. We may have been taught at church to fear God in a very ungodly way. Let's examine a few verses to help clear some things up.

We have taught in many nations on this very topic of how incredibly loving the Father is. Many times when it comes to talking about hindrances, we will have people approach us with this verse:

The fear of the LORD is the beginning of wisdom. (Psalm 111:10)

The word "fear" in this verse is the Hebrew word "yirah" which means not only "fear" but to be "in awe or reverence of." It is an understanding of the enormity of God, His incredible power, His omnipresence, and omnipotence. Rightly we should be in awe of Him because He is incredible in all of His ways. But the word "fear" in this verse is not fear as in terror or dread. It is not the type of fear that leads us to dread punishment or motivates us to try to live in perfection. That kind of fear is the word "phobos" from which we get the word "phobias." Look at the following verse but read it with the understanding that the word fear here is the Greek word "phobos."

> *There is no fear in love; but perfect love casts out fear, because fear involves punishment, and the one who fears is not perfected in love.*
>
> *(1 John 4:18)*

Every place in our heart that still greets God with fear does not yet know we are loved. His perfect love casts out all fears, phobias and expectations of punishment. You and I are caught up in a process of being perfected in love and having all the fear loved out of us.

Father God certainly does not want any of us to respond through fear in relationship with Him.

REFLECTION AND APPLICATION

Every place in our heart that still greets God with fear does not yet know we are loved.

1. Let's soak first today. While you are soaking ask the Holy Spirit to reveal to you anything or anyone that led you to believe that you are supposed to respond to God in fear. It could be your church background or denomination, or a relative who would emphasize fear of God in order to get you to behave a certain way. If any names or faces come to mind, spend some time releasing them into forgiveness. Destroy any IOUs that you have out toward them. Now, just soak in the love of the Father for 20 or 30 minutes.

2. Journal now and ask Papa a few questions such as:

    c. In what ways has my fear of You held me back from truly knowing You?

    b. Is there any memory that You want to heal today where that fear took hold?

    c. If so, ask Jesus where He was in that memory and what He wants to tell you about that situation.

Journal Notes

THE HINDRANCES OF STRIVING AND EARNING

Lesson Notes

Let's first look at definitions for striving and earning.

To Strive:

- *make great efforts to achieve or obtain something;*

- *struggle or fight vigorously*

To Earn:

- *gain or incur deservedly in return for one's behavior or achievements: "through the years she has earned affection and esteem."*

Many of us are stuck in a perpetual cycle with God of striving and earning. We may have learned early on in life that in order to receive love you need to behave a certain way. Or perhaps we heard a message at church that we interpreted as, "I need to fast more, pray more, read the Bible more, and then God will love me more!" We learn from a very young age that with correct behavior comes love and encouragement. Within the school system that process is reinforced with good grades for better work, getting picked first for the sports teams in the activities which you excel in, and having your art up in the hall way when you have done really well. All of those things in and of themselves are not evil or damaging, but they teach our hearts that in order to be noticed, picked or praised, we need to do better than everyone else.

> Many of us are stuck in a perpetual cycle with God of striving and earning. We may have learned early on in life that in order to receive love you need to behave a certain way.

The competition and rivalry only increases as we get older and go on to high school and university and eventually enter a profession. An internal engine of strife is embedded deep into our hearts through this process. Then, our hearts begin to strive toward God. Upon getting saved, we continue to bring our issues to church with us and into our relationship with God as well. We feel pressured to study more, take more Bible courses, fast here and there, and even soak, but all with the underlying current of, "If I do this He will love me more, it will make Him proud, and I can earn His approval."

There are many ungodly beliefs tied up in the way we relate to God. You simply cannot earn a free gift, and yet we still strive for His love! We try to get our acts together and "do" all the right things to prove ourselves worthy to be chosen, but He actually chose you before the creation of the world. (Yes! You were already chosen even when you were still caught up in all of your junk!))

These cycles of striving and earning keep us in a hamster wheel of stress and effort. God, however, desires that we would learn to rest, allow Him to pour into us and heal us, and then follow His leading throughout the day. Then we fast (to build hunger for God), and we pray because we can't wait to talk to Him. We also read the Word because we want to really know Him. Both striving and earning suck the life out of relationships and make them about marking a tally and keeping score. We want what we deserve for the hours spent in "spiritual pursuit." As a result, we cannot rest.

When we are in striving mode, we have a hard time receiving and then look for the next new thing to excel at in order to win God's favor, and the favor of man as well.

He chose you before the creation of the world.

REFLECTION AND ACTIVATION

1. Ask the Holy Spirit the following questions:

    a. In what areas of my life am I trying to earn Your love?

    b. Where did I learn to strive?

    c. When do I most often start to strive or earn?

2. Take your journal to where you are going to soak.

3. Start your soaking time by praying a prayer of forgiveness toward those people or institutions that taught you to strive for notice or love.

4. Now say another quick prayer something like this: "Father, please forgive me for striving and trying to earn your love and affection. I recognize this cycle in my life and ask you to break it today in Jesus' name. Today I choose to receive Your unconditional love as the free gift that it is and I invite you to begin the process of teaching me to rest in You. Amen."

5. Now soak for 20 or 30 minutes and keep inviting Him to come and wash away all striving.

6. Journal any insights He reveals to you.

Today I choose to receive Your unconditional love as the free gift that it is and I invite you to begin the process of teaching me to rest in You.

Journal Notes

THE HINDRANCE OF UNGODLY BELIEFS

Lesson Notes

Let's start by defining what we are talking about here. An ungodly belief (or UGB, as they say in the inner healing biz) is something that appears to be absolutely true based on the facts of your experience, but is absolutely false based on the truth of God's Word. UGBs are a very effective tactic of the enemy to rob life from us. They keep our wheels spinning and our hearts reeling in order to keep us from moving forward in the truth of God's love for us. They are lies, and we need to recognize them as such, but sometimes they are difficult to isolate and destroy on our own. I think part of the reason for that difficulty is that we have believed them for so long that they have become our "truth." Also, many times there is some sliver of truth in them and so we can't clearly see where the reality of experience gets twisted into a UGB. We get UGBs mainly from five key places:

An "ungodly belief" is something that appears to be absolutely true based on the facts of your experience, but is absolutely false based on the truth of God's Word.

1. Life's experiences.

2. Family heritages. We inherit our parent's views of life, and their prejudices.

3. Repetition. If you hear the same thing enough times eventually you begin to believe it is true. For example, while growing up, your parents or teachers called you stupid or lazy. If you hear that lie enough, eventually it becomes believable to you even though it is not the truth.

4. Negative thinking. We can be so critical of ourselves on a regular basis that we start to believe the lies our self-criticism produces.

5. The world's perspective. The world's way of thinking often influences us and we adopt UGBs from a mindset we were never meant to entertain. The popular media tells us what is beautiful and we agree; they tell us what is successful and we agree; and eventually we have a whole set of lies running in the background of our Christian journey.

Allow me to give you an example of the forming of a UGB. The first time I heard this teaching on UGBs, God highlighted in my life the following UGB that was established in my mind:

"If I allow God close enough to love me then He will leave me. Therefore, it's safer to never go there and not get abandoned."

Scripture says He will never leave me nor forsake me... He is who He says He is, and He's faithful.

Now that particular UGB was given lots of strength from life's experiences! I had loved my Dad and he killed himself. I loved my first husband and he left me for someone else. My heart screamed, "You will not survive God leaving you so just don't go there!" The problem, of course, is that my experience and my UGB don't line up with the truth of God's Word! Scripture says He will never leave me nor forsake me. Sometimes life says one thing and God says another, and the trick is to jump into God with both feet and trust that He is who He says He is, and that He's faithful.

UGBs can rob life from you in many areas. You may not believe you are loved or can be loved. As a result, you can possibly become a hard-hearted person who learns to survive... just like I did.

For as [a man] thinks in his heart, so he is. (Proverbs 23:7 NKJV)

I remember one day I was getting ready to teach on UGBs at an Encounter Weekend and I heard God say:

"What you say with your mouth today,
will determine what you believe tomorrow.
What you believe in your heart today,
will determine what you become tomorrow."

This topic of UGBs is much bigger than we can fully cover in one day's devotional. I always want to give credit where credit is due, and this teaching and revelation on UGBs belongs to Betsy and Chester Kylstra. The UGB teaching has brought such revelation and healing to me that it would be hard to overstate it. My intention today, however, is to take this little bit of understanding and focus it on lies that rob us of our relationship with Father God. I will post the Kylstras' materials in the recommended readings section at the back of this study so you can pursue this further, and I strongly recommend that you do, as it will be life to you.

Here are a few examples of some UGBs that relate to God:

I am not worthy to receive anything from God.

If I love God He will leave me.

If I fully give my life to Him He will make me be a missionary in Guam.

REFLECTION AND ACTIVATIONS

At the end of this section, you will see a work space that says UGB, with a space to write, then below it, GB (Godly Belief) and a space to write.

1. Ask God what UGBs you have believed about Him or who you are in Him that has hindered your relationship with Him. Write each UGB on a separate UGB line.

2. For each UGB read through the following prayer:

Confess

"Lord, I confess my sin of believing the lie that _____ (be specific)."

Forgive and repent

"I choose to forgive you, _____ (people who contributed to your forming this ungodly belief) for _____ (be specific- i.e. the words you spoke over me, for letting me down, etc).

What you say with your mouth today will determine what you believe tomorrow.

What you believe in your heart today will determine what you become tomorrow.

Lord, bring your healing touch to the hurt in my heart that led to my believing this lie.

"I repent and ask you to forgive me, Lord, for receiving this ungodly belief; for living my life based on it, and for any way I have judged others because of it. I receive your forgiveness."

Renounce

"I renounce and break my agreement with this ungodly belief and with all powers of darkness behind this belief.

"I choose to accept, believe and receive the godly belief that _____

_____."

Journal any more insights the Father shows you.

_____

_____

Lord, bring your healing touch to the hurt in my heart that led to my believing this lie.

Now spend some time soaking and let God talk to you about the Godly Belief. After soaking, grab this guide again and ask God for the Godly Belief to counter the UGB and then write it in the space provided.

Going forward as you start your study for the day, declare your Godly Beliefs about God out loud before doing your daily reading. If you do that for the remainder of this study, you will discover that those old UGBs about God have been dug up and completely removed.

UGB _____

GB _____

UGB _____

GB _____

UGB _____

GB _____

Journal notes

THE HINDRANCES OF COMPETITION AND RIVALRY

Lesson Notes

It appears that competition and rivalry have been around since the very beginning of time. Look through the beginning of the Old Testament to the end of the New Testament and examples are all over the place. Cain and Abel, Jacob and Esau, Joseph and his brothers, all the way through to the disciples – it's rampant! Why is it a hindrance for catching God's heart for us? There are a couple of different ways this robs us.

First of all, when we choose to participate in competition and rivalry we are unable to cheer on those around us with a pure heart because other people's successes become more about our own failures. In the face of their joy we feel robbed somehow. We are not created to live like this! With a clean heart, we are meant to celebrate with those who are celebrating and remain free from any "but what about me, God" pity parties lurking under the surface.

God has not forgotten you. He took the time to number the hairs on your head; He has written all of your days in His books; He knows the plans He has for you! How is it, then, that we lose sight of His goodness and faithfulness in the face of the success of others? It is because we listen to competition and rivalry that produces striving and performance. As a result, we never learn to rest in God's goodness, denying that we will see the fullness of all that He has for us.

"For I know the plans that I have for you,'" declares the LORD, "plans for welfare and not for calamity to give you a future and a hope."

(Jeremiah 29:11)

God has not forgotten you. He took the time to number the hairs on your head; He has written all of your days in His books; He knows the plans He has for you!

No one can steal your destiny from you except you! If you are letting God love you, mold you, change you, heal you, and prepare you for what He has for you, then you don't need to worry! God's ability to bless you beyond measure far outweighs the enemy's ability to rob from you. If you live life comparing yours with what others seem to be "getting" or even "getting away with" it will never lead to fruitfulness and life. This type of focus will open the door to frustration and more comparison. If God is who He says He is, and He is, then we need to learn to rest and believe that He actually is in control. We need to believe that He really does see everything, that there really is a plan, and that His plan is to bless us. In that belief we can remain in an attitude of rest and peace and not strive or perform. We will then live in joy knowing we are in good hands, receiving the fullness of abundant life.

REFLECTION AND ACTIVATION

God's ability to bless you beyond measure far outweighs the enemy's ability to rob from you.

1. If you know there was favoritism in your family growing up, then in your own words take a few minutes to release forgiveness to your parents or grandparents and the favored siblings. Hand over those situations to Papa God, and then pray this prayer:

    "Father, I recognize that I have felt in competition with _____ for your affections. I have reacted to this inwardly/outwardly in the following ways _____ and I ask you to forgive me. I know you have more than enough love to go around and that you are not comparing us but loving us fully just as we are. Lord, I ask that you would help me guard against competition and rivalry. I do not want to be that person anymore. I ask you to help me learn to rest in your love and lay down all striving and performance. I know you are faithful to complete what you have begun in me so I thank you and choose to trust you with this also, Papa. Amen."

2. Grab your pillow and soaking music and allow the Lord to wash over you. If He brings up some memories to heal, then just invite Jesus into each memory and ask Him to show you or tell you where He is and what He is doing in that moment. You might want to write down any fresh revelation you receive when you are finished soaking so you don't forget!

Journal Notes

_____
_____
_____
_____
_____
_____
_____
_____
_____
_____
_____
_____
_____
_____
_____
_____
_____
_____
_____
_____
_____
_____

THE HINDRANCE OF ATTEMPTING TO EARN GOD'S LOVE

Lesson Notes

Since being stuck in striving and performance is such a hindrance to our relationship with God, we're going to camp here for a while.

Consider this: striving and performance is the engine, if you will, which runs on all different kinds of fuel. The "fuel" we are going to tackle today is the whole area of attempting to earn God's love and favor. Again, we perform for all different reasons and often for many reasons that have all merged into one response – performance. My hope is that by separating them out and looking at the different fuels one by one, we will choke off the engine that keeps us running for God rather than resting and working with Him.

I remember when God brought this issue of earning His love home to me in a tangible way. I really struggled as a child to feel noticed or loved and that left me with a whole set of UGBs centered on striving and earning love. As a result, it took a good fifteen years after getting saved and ten years into the Father Heart message until the Lord began to focus on my motivation for service. At this time in my life, when I was not traveling, I would spend four or five hours a day with God in my "God room" just hanging out, journaling, soaking, praying, singing, and digging through the Word.

Striving and performance is a hindrance to our relationship with God. We perform for all different reasons rather than resting and working with Him.

Each day at some point during those hours I would begin to journal and I would always begin with the same question. I still frequently ask this question: "Papa, what do You want to say to me today?" One day I heard this: "I love you and I'm proud of you." He then went on to say other things but those words of life rested in my heart and brought healing. The next day as I had my time with Him, I asked the same questions, and He said again, "I love you and I'm proud of you." I remember thinking, "Umm, You said that already, Lord, but I'll write it down if you like." Well, several weeks down the line, EVERY DAY when I would go to journal, He would begin the same way, "I love you and I'm proud of you," and then He would say other things.

I became incredibly frustrated with this. Part of me was thinking, "Obviously I am making the whole thing up and I am so unoriginal that I can't even come up with something new everyday!" Another argument flowing through my mind was, "it's either the aforementioned unoriginality or I am so dense God needs to tell me the same thing 20 or 30 times to get it in my head – either of which can't be good!" Of course, God wasn't going for my head. He was aiming for my heart.

The Lord said to me:
"I love you and I'm proud
of you."

Fast forward two months with the same thing being said everyday and I am convinced I no longer hear God and my brain is stuck in a mental ditch, regurgitating the same dated message. This was my frame of mind on my way to minister for a weekend at a fantastic church. At this point, I had only been traveling full-time for a year or two, and this particular church was the largest one to which I had ever been invited to teach. Usually, I was invited to speak to the young adults and the youth, but on this occasion the senior pastor invited me to speak on Sunday morning. According to the associate pastor, this rarely happened.

A few months prior I had been asking God about how He would like me to prepare to speak when invited to each church. He had asked me to trust Him to give me relevant massages and to focus on a prepared life rather than prepared massages. Most often, that left me completely dependent on a "now" word, rather than a prepared word. Going into the weekend I had heard from the Lord what to do Friday night and Saturday night and even Sunday night, but I did not know what His plan was for Sunday morning. Of course, the problem with that was Sunday morning was the one I was most stressed about.

On Sunday morning I was driving to church with the senior pastors and completely stressed out of my mind as I still had no idea what I was speaking on. I couldn't hear anything from God regarding what to do and I didn't want to just fall back on what I "could" speak on. I wanted to honor my agreement with God. On top of that, I was pretty sure from some of his comments that the pastor wanted to know what I planned to speak about. I didn't think he would be encouraged by a rant about how God and I had made an agreement but now He isn't talking and I think I may just end up on stage in front of 1,100 people and just smile because at this point I've got NOTHING!!!!! As we got closer to the church I tried to settle myself in the back of the SUV. In resignation and frustration I asked, "Papa, is there anything You want to say to me this morning?" And He said, "Yes." My heart leapt! I was thinking, "Finally, the download has arrived! I am not sunk, I won't be kicked off the platform, and I am not going to fail in front of all these people that I respect! "What is it Lord? What do you want to share today?" And the Lord said, "AJ, I love you and I'm proud of you."

He loves us and nothing we do will make Him change his mind.

That was it. Nothing more followed. I nearly cried. I prayed for the rapture all while appearing calm for the benefit of the pastors in the front seat. Are you with me so far? Do you feel the tension? We arrive at the church and walk up to the front row. Sitting there in reserved seats are two people that God has really used to help parent me for many years previous, Fred and Sharon Wright. They, along with John and Carol, had released me into full-time ministry. Fred had written a recommendation letter to all of the churches within our network commending me and encouraging them to bring me in to speak. Here they were on the front row about to be disappointed in me. Surely, I was about to fail spectacularly. I wanted to go up and tell them, "Ok, just so you know, I don't hear God anymore and I just keep making up the same things in my head and I'm about to get up there and embarrass myself and probably you, as well!" But there was no time to get that out as worship had begun and as all those around me worshiped with abandon, I raised my hands and internally begged again for rapture.

Suddenly, Fred was standing before me with tears in his eyes. I looked at him wondering why he was crying and he said, "AJ, I am just standing here talking to God and all I can hear is His heart over you and He keeps saying the same things: "Tell her I love her and I'm proud of her." In that moment the penny dropped. I am not making it up; He loves me and He is proud of me no matter what I do or don't do. Regardless if I fail or succeed. If I preach an awesome message or a simple one or just stand there and smile, it doesn't matter. I don't have to earn His love or approval, it is already mine!!!! In that moment as I am being introduced, Papa God in His faithfulness dropped one verse in my spirit.

After being baptized, Jesus came up immediately from the water; and behold, the heavens were opened, and He saw the Spirit of God descending as a dove and lighting on Him, and behold, a voice out of the heavens said, "This is My beloved Son, in whom I am well-pleased."

(Matthew 3:16)

I spoke that morning on a love that isn't earned – it is received. Jesus had done no miracles when the Father proclaimed that He was His beloved Son in whom He was well pleased! He hadn't raised the dead or fed 5,000. He hadn't healed anyone or preached the Sermon on the Mount. He had done NOTHING! He simply was. And in that place, the Father loved Him fully just as He does you and me. "This is my beloved Son in whom I am well pleased." My heart caught truth that morning as a simple message brought me life…"You don't need to earn anything. I don't require your performance, just rest in this truth – just as you are right now you are loved and I'm proud of you." I return to that truth often, whenever I feel the striving begin to show its ugly head. I return to the truth of Love, a truth that cannot be earned because it is a free gift that already cost God everything to give.

...and behold, a voice out of the heavens said, "This is My beloved Son, in whom I am well-pleased." (Matthew 3:16)

Jesus had done no miracles when the Father proclaimed that He was His beloved Son in whom He was well pleased!

REFLECTION AND ACTIVATION

1. Spend some time journaling with God around these questions:

   a. Papa in what ways am I trying to earn your love?

b. What needs to change for me to be able to rest in your love?

2. Now go ahead and spend some time soaking and just rest in that love. Don't pray other than to invite Him to come and pour in His love; then rest.

Journal Notes

_____

_____

_____

_____

_____

_____

_____

_____

_____

_____

_____

_____

_____

_____

_____

_____

_____

_____

_____

_____

_____

_____

Journal Notes

EXPERIENCE

Welcome to Week Five. We are going to spend this week looking at some of our life's experiences and how those experiences have helped us shape our view of God.

Our experiences growing up in the home we did, with the parents, grandparents, and authority figures we had, and in the churches and schools we attended, have all colored our view of God in some way. Some experiences paint accurate representations of God's love for us and others don't.

We need to set some ground rules right from the start. Firstly, we need to stay well-practiced at releasing and forgiving. Your parents really have done the very best they could with what they had been given. Hurting people hurt people, and that's just the way it is. They probably parented with the parenting skills they were parented with. Our parents were not perfect; just as we are not, nor will we ever be.

I think it's helpful from the onset to release them from the expectation that we required of them to know the right thing to do in every situation, or respond perfectly in every circumstance. We need to be very careful of our heart's response to pain and memories. It would be wise for us to withhold judgments and statements like, "I'll never do that to my kid," or, "I'll never be like my Mom and/or Dad." Those types of statements arise out of judgment and their fruit produces exactly the thing you have hated in your life. Don't believe me? Look at this:

> *You, therefore, have no excuse, you who pass judgment on someone else, for at whatever point you judge the other, you are condemning yourself, because you who pass judgment do the same things.*
>
> *(Romans 2:1 NIV)*

I have lost count of how many people we have prayed with who are repeating the very things they hated in their childhood. The reason for

Our experiences growing up in the home we did have all colored our view of God in some way. Some experiences paint accurate representations of God's love for us and others don't.

the repeat cycle is because they judged their parents, pastors or authority figures for the things that were done to them in their growing up years. Trust me, you don't want to go there.

Ground Rules for This Week

Ground Rule #1: While God is revealing keys to you to release you into a deeper knowledge of Him, do not judge those who misrepresented God's Father heart toward you knowingly or unknowingly. We are all on a journey of knowing His Father heart toward us and then reflecting it, or representing it to the world around us. We don't do that perfectly yet, nor did those who came before you.

Ground Rule #2: Be open to God showing you the roots of your issues even if they are things you never considered before! Your "Father concept" was built into you from any number of influential sources in your life. However, if you have the "fruit" of building walls between you and God, then you have the "root" that those walls sprung out of. It's only through allowing God to reveal His truth to our hearts, along with uprooting the negative roots, that we can destroy those walls for good. Don't stir issues up yourself, but allow the Holy Spirit to speak truth to you.

Why are Fathers so pivotal in our lives?

For a number of reasons, actually. If your Dad was a reasonably whole man, he will have been able to call you to life, to live to the fullest and expect good things, and to speak significance into your very core. Those messages of approval and significance that we receive as children begin to build our personality and character. If somehow we missed the message that we are loved, accepted, significant, valued, and wanted, we often end up with any number of personality and character issues that stem from that very lack. Not only can we end up perpetually insecure and second-guessing ourselves, but we may also be overbearing, as if to prove to the world that we have a right to be here and that we have value.

How we see Father God determines whether we can receive love, security, acceptance, rest, comfort, provision, and healing in the Father's

If somehow we missed the message that we are loved, accepted, significant, valued, and wanted, we often end up with any number of issues that stem from that very lack.

Presence. God's desire for you is to know in your depths that you are wanted, you were planned, you bring Him joy, you have value and you belong to Him. Therefore, the purpose of this week is to look at any place in our childhood and past where we received a message that was contrary to how God actually feels about us.

The dictionary defines a Father as "the person we get our significance from." My prayer for you this week is that you will begin to receive the significance, value, love and honor that the Father has wanted for you from the very beginning.

As He begins to reveal any false concepts about Himself and every image that has misrepresented Him, allow Him to heal and set you free. He will breakdown the strongholds where our struggles have kept Him at arms' length and under suspicion as we look at Him through the colored lenses of our pasts.

This week we will be spending one day on each of the six father types that tend to form roadblocks in our ability to see Father God as He actually is. With each Father Type, we will be looking at how that Father Type is defined, how it affects our view of God, and how we function in relation to God as a result. We will begin to remove the lenses from our eyes and lives that have clouded the Father's love toward us.

God's desire for you is to know in your depths that you are: wanted, you were planned, you bring Him joy, you have value and you belong to Him.

THE PASSIVE FATHER

Lesson Notes

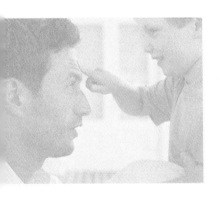

It is that extravagant love that calls us to life and destiny.

The Passive Father is characterized primarily by the following:

- He is not home even when he is home.

- He is not intimate or part of our lives.

- He is not able to express emotions and may have a hard time saying "I love you."

- He may not be comfortable with physical affection.

- He is shut down emotionally.

I have met many people over the years who have never heard the words, "I love you," from their dad. Their dads were shut down, greeting them with handshakes instead of hugs, and they never showed emotion. They were not abusive or aggressive, merely unable to accurately represent the extravagant love that Father God has for us, and it is that extravagant love that calls us to life and destiny. Simply put, undemonstrated love, wounds us. Often the absence of something good can speak louder than the presence of something bad.

How does our experience with a Passive Father affect our view of God? We usually think things such as:

- We may know that He loves us but we believe it is from a distance.

- We walk by faith that God loves us.

- We do not think we can experience the love of the Father.

- We think God is not interested in our lives!

As a result we tend to become people who learn how to cope. We are survivors who are numb to the love that the Father is trying to pour out on us because we don't know what to do with it! We often have a difficult time expressing love ourselves.

Here's the good news: Papa God is not actually the way He has been represented to you! He is not passive about you or about His love for you! He wove you together in your mother's womb. He is not distant – He is right up close! He has counted all the hairs on your head and you have to get up close and personal to do that. If you don't believe me, try it with a stranger today and see what kind of reaction you get! It's intimate, it's caring, and for some of us it takes a really long time!

REFLECTION AND ACTIVATION

1. Start today by forgiving you dad, mom, pastor, head master, aunt, teacher, etc. for any way they misrepresented Father God as being passive about your life.

2. If Father brings up any specific memories that helped reinforce the perception of a passive Father, just ask Jesus where He was in that memory and what message He wanted you to receive in that moment.

3. Ask Father God what He wants you to know about His extravagant love for you. Journal His response.

4. If possible, try to soak for 30 minutes or more and just pray a simple prayer like this: "Father, please rewrite the truth of Your love on my heart this day." Journal, Journal, Journal.

God is not passive about you or about His love for you! He wove you together in your mother's womb.

Journal Notes

THE ABSENT FATHER

Lesson Notes

The Absent Father is characterized primarily by the following: he is absent because of death, divorce, abandonment, or working too much.

I really struggled with this view of God as a result of my childhood. Between how much Dad worked when I was little, and him being shut off when he got home, we had little contact with him. He would come home from the office and go downstairs to his drafting room, and that was it. Sometimes he would just sit in front of the TV until He fell asleep from exhaustion, but either way he was not available to me. When my parents divorced, I didn't see my Dad for a long time (which is what I wanted at the time) but it still reinforced that abandonment. Finally, in 1991 when he killed himself after just four or five brief healthy years of building relationship with each other, my perceptions were solidified: Dads leave; they just leave.

So, how do we tend to respond? Oftentimes we transfer that view of fathers onto God and we think things like: "If I really love God, He will leave," and we become afraid to risk relationship with God because in pursuing relationship we fear that rejection will find us. We don't really know what to do with a dad and some of us are not really sure we even need one. If we have never known our earthly father then it can become very difficult to relate to the message of a loving Heavenly Father. It's like trying to describe the color green to a blind person.

If we have never known our earthly father then it can become very difficult to relate to the message of a loving Heavenly Father. It's like trying to describe the color green to a blind person.

Therefore, we often become very intense and serious even from a very young age. We can tend to be cautious, independent and self-reliant. When we should have been playing, we were surviving. As a result, we potentially become very angry people under the surface and either lash out or internalize it. The experience of an absent father is one that leaves us feeling absolutely alone no matter how many people are in the room.

Your father was supposed to speak love and acceptance into your very core. It was his job to see your destiny and to speak life into it. So, sometimes when we have grown up with this Father Type, we can feel the need to prove that we are even allowed to be here! There is a part of our soul designed by God to be activated by our dads. This process of activation causes us to feel legitimate, but when the father is absent, this part of us is underdeveloped. As a result, we must activate ourselves and ultimately fight feelings of illegitimacy because something deep within still feels out of order.

So, what do we do? We start with forgiving our Dads for not being there, for not calling us to life or speaking life to our destiny, for not being available or around when we needed them. We thank them for doing the best they could with what they had to give no matter how good or bad that "best" was, and we release them from our judgment. Then we invite Father God to come and write on our hearts with His Fathering love.

Invite Father God to come and write on your heart with His Fathering love.

REFLECTION AND ACTIVATION

1. Grab your pen and get ready to journal. Ask Papa these questions:

   a. Daddy, I have learned to survive. What do you want me to know about the things You have put in me that you are beginning to activate and call to life.

   b. In what ways do I internalize or act out the frustration I have felt in not being called to life? What do You want to do with those things?

2. Now, grab your pillow and get comfortable. When you lay down, start by asking the Lord to wash over you and then invite Him in your own words to call you to life.

Journal Notes

_____

_____

_____

_____

_____

_____

_____

_____

_____

_____

_____

_____

_____

_____

_____

_____

_____

_____

_____

_____

_____

_____

THE PERFORMANCE ORIENTED FATHER

Lesson Notes

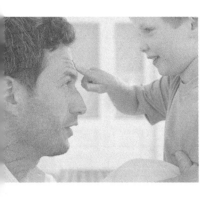

When we place a performance oriented view onto God we believe that God only values us for what we can do for Him and not for relationship.

The Performance Oriented Father is characterized by the following:

- He values strict obedience.

- Has high standards and demands.

- He rewards for fulfilling expectations / he shows disapproval or disappointment for not meeting them.

- He may devalue you when you fail.

When we place that view onto God, we believe that God only values us for what we can do for Him and not for relationship. We can never pray enough, fast enough, serve enough, or lead enough people to the Lord to satisfy that view of God. We often feel like no matter what, "in the end I fail." At the end of a cycle of trying our best, we quit, give up and shut down early so we don't have to compete. We are trying to earn a love that is a free gift, and it keeps us running like a hamster on a wheel as we try to maintain appearances and keep all our balls in the air. Deep inside we believe we can never measure up, and so we live with a constant feeling and expectation of failure in every situation.

So what do we become as a result of this view of God? We become people who strive for attention and affirmation. We are driven to be the best in order to impress the world, or at least our part of it. We believe our value is in what we do, not who we are, and so we are constantly pushing to succeed. We attempt to look good on the outside even if we are dying on the inside. It's far more important to look "right" than to actually be right.

One of the root causes of depression is being raised in a performance-oriented household. In that type of household, the appearance of things matter much more than how you feel or how you are doing as a child. In America, 80% of pastors' kids have been treated for depression. I know it's shocking, but I'll tell you something, it's not just the parents adding that pressure on the preachers' kids (PKs) – it's us! Oftentimes the congregation has unreasonable expectations of pastors' kids, telling them to be a role model and that others are watching; examining their every move under a magnifying glass... they never had a chance! Can we please extend them some grace to live a normal life without our "critical eye" on their every move?

Strangely enough, for those of us raised in a performance-oriented (PO) home, we will not only have unreasonable expectations of ourselves but of others as well. That being so, whatever we have to do to feel good about ourselves is what we will then require of others in order for us to respect them. We just keep living in and passing on the pressure. We pass on the sin of perfectionism. Think about this; if the Father were only interested in our performance, the prodigal son story would read like a rejection nightmare. The story doesn't end like that because He is sincerely interested in us as His beloved and His love for us is unconditional.

God is sincerely interested in us as His beloved and His love for us is unconditional.

REFLECTION AND ACTIVATION

1. Ask Father the following questions and journal the insights He gives you:

    a. In what ways do I look at myself through the eyes of performance orientation?

    b. Where did I learn PO? (parents, church, school, etc.)

    c. What do you want to do to unwind it in me?

WEEK 5 - DAY 3

2. Now let's pray another little prayer of releasing anyone the Lord showed us as contributors to a PO view of God. It may sound something like this:

"Father, I forgive _____ for every way they misrepresented Your love for me. I release them from my judgments and recognize and thank them for doing the best they could with what they had. Now, Father, would You come and unwind in me all the ways of performance orientation that have been present in my thinking and in my doing. I know that You love me just the way I am and there is not a single thing I can do to make You love me more! Thank You, Papa; please help my heart to receive this truth!"

3. Enjoy a soaking time (30 minutes or more if possible) and invite His love again to come and wash over you and unwind you.

Journal Notes

_____

_____

_____

_____

_____

_____

_____

_____

_____

_____

_____

_____

_____

_____

_____

THE AUTHORITARIAN FATHER

Lesson Notes

The "Authoritarian Father" is characterized by the following:

- He is a legalist.

- There is very little love in the law.

- He emphasizes the truth and the letter of the law instead of relationship.

- He does not let you become your own person or develop your own individuality.

- He is more comfortable with obedience and truth than with love and intimacy.

- He doesn't know how to express the love he feels.

As a result of an authoritarian view of God, we tend to become Christians who are intolerant of other Christians who don't think or act as we do.

It we have this view of God, then we likely believe that God is as impatient for us as we to get it together. Many are convinced that He only cares that we follow the rules and not about our feelings or motives, He just wants obedience. With this kind of frame of reference, you may think that you are not allowed to ask God questions, or have a conversation. You might think that your only response option is "Yes!" … and it better be enthusiastic too!

As a result of this view we tend to become Christians who are intolerant of other Christians who don't think or act as we do. We judge them by a clear set of rules in our heads and find them lacking. If we are responsible for something going wrong, we quickly look for someone else to blame so when God's legalistic hammer falls it doesn't hit us. At the root of this response is an ungodly tormenting fear of God. That fear, though well hidden in legalism and rules, will keep us from ever letting down the walls and allowing Father God to get close. No one in their right mind goes into a room and looks around for the scariest person they can find to befriend them. Therefore, if life has taught us to fear God like that, there will always be some kind of protector within us that puts up walls around our heart faster than we can take them down. It is hard to draw close to God or have Him draw close to us with this type of defense mechanism.

Read Jeremiah 31:3 – it proclaims that He has loved us with an everlasting love and draws us with loving-kindness. We need our heart healed up in order to respond!

REFLECTION AND ACTIVATION

1. Ask Father the following questions and journal the answers:

    a. Who has taught my heart to fear you through representing you as an authoritarian?

    b. Has part of me been rebuilding walls even while I desire to tear them down between us?

    c. What truth do You want to speak to me about this today?

2. Let's pray another prayer of forgiveness so that we can receive what God wants to do in us today. In your own words pray something like this:

    "Father, I forgive _____ for every way they misrepresented Your love for me. I release them from my judgments and recognize and thank them for doing the best they could with what they had. Now, Father, would You come and pull down all the walls that I have built to hide from You because of fear. Thank you, Papa; please help my heart to receive this truth!"

Jeremiah 31:3 proclaims that He has loved us with an everlasting love and draws us with loving-kindness.

3. Grab your pillow and soaking music and have a lovely time soaking while asking God to bring down your walls in His timing.

Journal Notes

_____

_____

_____

_____

_____

_____

_____

_____

_____

_____

_____

_____

_____

_____

_____

_____

_____

_____

_____

_____

THE ABUSIVE FATHER

Lesson Notes

Abuse from a father figure destroys our trust in male authority and our healthy image of a loving God.

Characteristics of the Abusive Father - The Abusive Father inflicts deep emotional pain by means of one or more of the following:

- Physical abuse may come from harsh unjust punishments, beatings, slaps to the face.

- Emotional abuse may occur from harsh or fearful tones of voice, devaluing words, demeaning looks, or from not meeting the basic emotional needs of a child for expressed love, security, praise, and purpose.

- Sexual Abuse may occur from any kind of wrong touching within the areas of the sexual organs, from improper sexually explicit language, or from seductive looks or activities (ie. inviting a child to look at pornography).

It stands to reason that any kind of abuse from a father figure results in some of the deepest wounds a child can receive. It destroys our trust in male authority and our healthy image of a loving God. We view God as a big cop in the sky or a God of wrath, and conclude that father figures are to be avoided and feared. Again, no one wants to be in relationship with someone they are afraid of. We may fear that if we were to allow God to draw close He will hurt us, so we choose to barricade our hearts. I remember when I was young I could not imagine a happy, friendly, or loving God. My cousin, aunt and uncle and grandparents had often tried to explain what He is like but my heart just couldn't make the leap. It didn't make sense to me that there is a loving God out there when my world looked the way it did. Then there was the other side I would ponder, "IF there is this loving God, then why hasn't He protected me?" To be honest, I was angry; really angry, as I didn't understand that it was Satan who was the mastermind behind my childhood pain. Neither did I comprehend that the people who had hurt me had made their own choices to do so. All I could think was, "Well if a God does exist then I hate Him."

I don't think it's uncommon for those who have suffered any kind of abuse to be angry and need somewhere to focus that anger. Some internalize it, others will externalize it, and still others, focus it all on one person… and for some that person is God.

I guarantee you that God is not the author of your childhood trauma. It was not His desire for you to suffer harm. There was nothing so flawed about you that you deserved to suffer the things that you did. You are not a bad person and God wants you free from all those feelings of shame, guilt and unworthiness. He longs to restore to you an accurate vision of yourself along with an accurate vision of Him. The good news is that you truly can let God in and allow Him to love you back to life. He will heal you inside and out. It is a well-known fact that many people abuse because they themselves also suffered abuse. My own father was abused by his mother. Although it doesn't excuse what he did to me and my family, it enabled me to extend lots of grace and mercy to him, and it made it easier to forgive him. He was trying to do the best he could with what he had. Unfortunately, sometimes his "best" just wasn't so great.

I know if you have been abused you likely find it really hard to trust people, just as I did. When you are healed, you will not do to others what was done to you. Most likely, God will use other healed up moms and dads to breathe life into you and begin to heal your heart, but you have to let them in. I understand what a scary prospect that is. But, I encourage you to ask God who you should trust, and allow those people to begin to re-parent you. It took me quite a while to begin letting in those parents that God sent my way, but am I ever glad I did. They really did love me back to life. If we choose to keep rejecting authority figures and father figures that are safe, we will find that we

The good news is that you truly can let God in and allow Him to love you back to life.

are thwarted in our spiritual, emotional, and behavioral development. We need to make room for healthy, loving, and wise spiritual parents to call us to life.

REFLECTION AND ACTIVATION

As we begin reflecting today, I want to encourage you to take a few moments to reflect on one other type of abuse that is prevalent in the church today: spiritual abuse. Sadly, there are many leaders who through their own woundedness are wounding others. That may take many different forms, from taking advantage or using people to meet the needs of their own ministry; to control and manipulation to have their own needs met. Sometimes we find it difficult to release the "Man" or "Woman of God" not only because we expect better from them, but because they are representatives of God to us! The fact is they are not perfect. Every person, no matter how long they have served the Lord, will make mistakes, hurt people intentionally or unintentionally, and make decisions that affect a wider circle then they anticipated. Are they still entitled to your forgiveness? Yes; they qualify under being human. Even the most wonderful of leaders will occasionally let you down and you need to be able to release them and keep moving toward God. I can promise you this: God will never let you down. He is consistent and faithful even when the best of men are not. Rest in that and allow him to restore your trust by trusting first in Him before anyone else.

God will never let you down. He is consistent and faithful even when the best of men are not.

1. Let's start by forgiving today... pray with me:

    "Father God, I forgive my dad, mom and anyone else in authority that misrepresented who You are to me and what Your love looks like for me. I release them from my judgments and my anger, and I tear up every I.O.U. I have been holding over them. I know we all do the best we can with what we have and I choose to let them go today. Daddy, I have been hiding from You out of fear, but today I ask that You would begin to take down my walls and love me back to life. I know You will be faithful to do this because You love me far more than I can even imagine at this point."

2. Spend time soaking in His love today. Don't do anything but lay there and invite Him to bathe you in His loving kindness and wash away the scars on your heart.

3. When you are done soaking, ask Papa what truths He wants to speak into your heart today and journal what He speaks.

Journal Notes

_____

_____

_____

_____

_____

_____

_____

_____

_____

_____

_____

_____

_____

_____

_____

_____

_____

_____

_____

_____

THE GOOD FATHER

Lesson Notes

Hurray! There are actually good fathers in this world! There is no doubt that being raised in a household with a healed dad is one of the best starts you can get. He has been able to speak love and security into you. His consistency in love made you secure and sure-footed on the path of life.

While having a good dad should lend us a head start in having a great image of a loving God, sometimes we get stuck in other places. We may feel that we do not need Father God because the role is already being filled so well. We may find in our Christian walk that we mostly relate and communicate with Jesus or the Holy Spirit but rarely with Father God. Or perhaps you struggle with guilt over being wounded by what seemed like a minor issue for others, but because your dad was so good you were really hurt when he missed that one game or recital as it seemed such a departure from the norm.

Scripture says there are no perfect fathers except Daddy God. So, we actually need to release our dads to be awesome, fantastic, great, loving dads without the pressure of having to be perfect. Then we need to allow Father God to have an active place of love and input in our everyday life without feeling guilty for desiring that. Even your awesome dad cannot fill your God-shaped hole, so free him from that expectation and let God be God for you in a new way.

Even your awesome dad cannot fill your God-shaped hole, so free him from that expectation and let God be God for you in a new way.

REFLECTION AND ACTIVATION

1. Let's pray first again today...

   "Father God, I thank you for my awesome dad. I recognize that he was not perfect just like I am not perfect, but I am so thankful for him. Lord, today I choose to release him from any judgments I have made against him and I release him from having to be my source of all comfort and wisdom. I ask You, Daddy God, to take that place. I look forward to this new journey into Your heart, God, and getting to know You as I let you into my life as a Father."

2. Soak in His love again today and then when you are done spend a few minutes journaling and asking God these questions:

   a. Daddy God, what childhood experiences with my dad have you uniquely designed for me to have insight into Your character?

   b. Daddy, what were some of Your favorite memories of mine with my dad?

Father God, I thank you for my awesome dad. I recognize that he was not perfect just like I am not perfect, but I am so thankful for him. I release him from having to be my source of all comfort and wisdom. I ask You, Daddy God, to take that place.

Journal Notes

THE PRODIGAL SON

One of the clearest visuals that we have in Scripture of God's Father heart toward us is in the story for the prodigal son in Luke 15. It's a story that many of us have read a hundred times and yet somehow our hearts often manage to miss its truths.

Let's start with the word "prodigal." The word prodigal means to be wasteful, reckless, and careless. We rightfully think of "wasteful" in a negative light in this context. But there is also wastefulness in the eyes of man that is actually a positive, holy, extravagance. One example of this is found in the life of Mary of Bethany when she poured out all her expensive oil upon Jesus. Individuals in the room thought it was wasteful but Jesus explained that it was her offering of worship for Him (John 12:3). Her extravagant gift was an expression of her deep love.

In the story of the prodigal son, we find his father being completely extravagant in kindness and what might even look like carelessness in His affection... but it was love – his father's love! This is a picture of Father's love for us. God gives Himself to us in extravagance and abandonment. It is Papa God's nature to give and keep giving, out of His abundant love for us.

Let's open up to Luke 15 and lay the ground-work for this week. Even though the parable starts with, "And a certain man had two sons..." I love the insight that Jack Frost brought to this passage when I heard him teach on it years ago. He asked the question, "How many sons are there in the prodigal son story?" We all responded "Two," as it says right there in verse 11. He waited a few moments and then pointed out, "There are three." He went on to explain: There is the younger son in the beginning of the story and the older son at the end, but the whole story is told by the Son in the center. Jesus is the Son in the center. In

In the story of the prodigal son, we find his father being completely extravagant in kindness and what might even look like carelessness in His affection… but it was love – his father's love!

red-letter editions, the whole story is in red because Jesus is telling it. Picture Jesus, the Son in the center, telling the parable; and He is saying, "This is what my Father is like." We know that Jesus knows the Father fully and that He would never lie to us about what He is like, so let's pray this prayer:

"Jesus, I invite You to come this week and write the truth on my heart about this extravagant love the Father has for me. I thank You that You have removed hindrances to knowing His love in my heart, and You have been stripping away every false perception of what He is like. I give You permission this week to bypass my head and to envelope my heart with the revelation of the Father's love. Amen. "

With that framework let's begin:

"And He said, "A man had two sons. The younger of them said to his father, 'Father, give me the share of the estate that falls to me.' And he divided his wealth between them." (Luke 15:11,12)

Right from the very beginning we see God's heart shining through. It sounds okay when you read, "Father, give me the share of the estate that falls to me." But in actual fact the sentiment might be better read: "Dad, I wish you were dead, I want my money." And as offensive as that request is, the father divides his estate to give the younger son what he asked for. Whenever I read this passage I remind myself to ask the Father only for what He desires for me to have and not just what I want to have out of my selfish desires. But, here we have the image of God in the person of the father in this story granting the request of an immature and confused kid. Then, right away in the following verses we see the same son strike his father's love again...

"And not many days later, the younger son gathered everything together and went on a journey into a distant country, and there he squandered his estate with loose living." (Luke 15:13)

To leave the country of your father's birth in those days was another massive slap in the face. In addition to all of that, the son's indulgence of selfish desires squandered his entire inheritance!

Jesus, I invite You to write the truth on my heart about this extravagant love the Father has for me.

"Now when he had spent everything, a severe famine occurred in that country, and he began to be in need. And he went and attached himself to one of the citizens of that country, and he sent him into his fields to feed swine.

"And he was longing to fill his stomach with the pods that the swine were eating, and no one was giving anything to him." (Luke 15:14-16)

I want you to imagine this for a moment. Here is a young man who was the son of a landowner with several slaves. He is accustomed to wealth, but because of his poor choices he finds himself only employable for one thing – feeding pigs. Imagine this imagery to a Jewish audience. A young Jewish guy feeding pigs! What do you think – good job or bad job? Bad, of course! And to top it all off he is in such a low place that he is looking at what pigs eat, which in my opinion looks like mud with chunks, and yet because of his condition, he is thinking, "Yummy!" Would you agree that the youngest son is in a very desperate place?

Sometimes the desperate place or severe famine in our lives has been allowed simply so we can realize we need to come home. I don't believe God orchestrates difficulty or pain, but I do think He will allow the impact and consequences of our decisions to make us uncomfortable enough that we start to head home in our hearts. And when we begin to head home to Jesus and the Father in our hearts, our feet will quickly follow!

That is the purpose of this study – allowing our feet to follow where our hearts have so desired to go. Some of us got no further away than the mud room; others got to the back yard; and still others made it down the road and over the mountains to another land entirely. It doesn't matter how far away we traveled; His loving, extravagant, lavishly forgiving heart toward us still cried out for our return! We are going to spend the next few days looking at that process of returning in our hearts and watching our feet follow.

It doesn't matter how far away we traveled, His loving, extravagant, lavishly forgiving heart toward us still cries out for our return!

WHAT AM I?

Lesson Notes

Luke 15:17 states, *"But when he came to his senses…"*

I love the first few words of verse 17. It reminds me to hope for those who I am waiting to see return to God because we have all done this at some point in our returning: come to our senses. Some of us can even remember the moment that we woke up in the middle of the life we were living, and said something like, "Hey, wait a minute; what am doing here? It was so much better with Papa; how did I get so far away? Can anyone show me the way home from here?"

The prodigal son is having one of those moments of revelation, as noted in verse 17, "But when he came to his senses, he said, 'How many of my father's hired men have more than enough bread, but I am dying here with hunger!" The paraphrase might be "Dude, what on earth am I thinking? There is a feast at home and life was good there; I mean, even the servants have everything they need!"

I think this is an interesting revelation. We are looking at two different categories of relationship in regards to the Father: 1) sons and 2) servants / or hired men. The son's revelation is that even those that are employed by the father have more than enough; yet, they are still clearly employees and not sons. Because we are provided for, even abundantly provided for, often we can live thinking that our hearts know we are sons – as though provision proves our heart's position. However, this verse says even those who are only as close as an em-

In God's economy even "slaves" are well provided for, but Father God wants so much more for you. He does not see you as a slave but as a son.

ployee; those who can follow instructions and serve well; will be fully provided for.

While it is encouraging to know that Papa will take care of us simply because we belong to Him, I want more than that - and I think He wants more for all of us. He calls us sons and He wants a full inheritance for us, not just a salary. As sons we have access to everything; yet as employees, access to both His heart and His resources are much more limited. This revelation of His goodness to even employees is what turned the younger son's heart back in the direction of the Father; it was the acknowledging of his Papa's generosity and goodness even to his slaves. In God's economy "slaves" are well provided for, but Father God wants so much more for you. He does not see you as a slave but as a son.

> *"I will get up and go to my father, and will say to him, 'Father, I have sinned against heaven, and in your sight; I am no longer worthy to be called your son; make me as one of your hired men.'"* (Luke 15:18-19)

I love the visual I get from this verse. What is the younger son doing here? Is he actually speaking to his father yet? No. He is practicing his apology speech! I don't know about you but I can certainly remember messing up so bad that I would practice my apology speech just to make sure it was convincing and full of impact. I remember even using a mirror while practicing for confirmation of the full effect! Here he is; he's ready, his heart has turned for home and his feet are getting ready to follow. It's really exciting, isn't it?

REFLECTION AND ACTIVATION

1. Let's begin by journaling today and asking Jesus to show us some pivotal moments in our walk with Him. Here are some questions.

   a. Lord, at what moment did You bring me to my senses and why then?

   b. Daddy, has my heart fully caught that You have much more for me than a kingdom salary; that You actually have a Kingdom inheritance with my name on it? How can I partner or position myself to better understand this revelation?

It is encouraging to know that Papa will take care of us simply because we belong to Him. He calls us sons and He wants a full inheritance for us.

2. Grab your pillow and soaking CD. Spend some time just resting in His Presence and inviting Him to begin to upgrade your internal understanding from employee to heir.

Journal Notes

_____

_____

_____

_____

_____

_____

_____

_____

_____

_____

_____

_____

_____

_____

_____

_____

_____

_____

_____

_____

_____

THE RETURN

Lesson Notes

My heart is full of hope that the full truth of these verses from Luke 15 will impact both your hearts and your walk with God in a very real way.

"So he got up and came to his father. But while he was still a long way off, his father saw him, and felt compassion for him, and ran and embraced him, and kissed him." (Luke 15:20)

So the son "got up and came to his father." He took the first step and headed his feet in the direction of his heart's desire. (You, too, have done that during this study.) He put action behind his heart, trusting that what had been stirring there concerning the goodness of his father was true. I love it! If I were to simplify my life's mission it would be: "To see the lost, the prodigals and the servants of God returning and finding themselves as heirs in the Father's heart." And what a return! Let's look at it piece by piece because it is SO good!

"But while he was still a long way off, his father saw him, and felt compassion for him." (20:b)

Think about this for a moment. The prodigal's father must have been diligently looking for him if he saw him while he was yet a long way off! He must have been outside scanning the horizon in expectation of the moment his son would come to his senses and return. I want you to imagine the emotion of a father longing for the return of his be-

Imagine the emotion of a father longing for the return of his beloved son as he regularly looks into the distance for his loved one's return. And there, in a moment of time, a dusty figure appears in the murky distance.

loved son, with enough emotion to keep that twice slapped-in-the-face father full of faith as he regularly looks into the distance for his loved one's return. And there, in a moment of time, a dusty figure appears in the murky distance.

Imagine the son, how tired he would be walking from one country to another in the Middle Eastern heat, with no bottled water, and not having eaten well in many moons. You can almost feel the energy expended just to make it that final short distance home. Imagine, also, the smell that would accompany this young fellow! Have you ever been near a pig farm? On a hot day you will know if you are within five miles of one because the smell is so pungent; and this poor fellow has been living in a pen with the pigs! No amount of cologne can help him now. Think about the stench of body odor from walking in all that heat with no deodorant to mask the scent. I see him like Pig-Pen from the Peanuts cartoon with a little cloud of his own dirt surrounding every movement. The father looks and sees his son and what rises up in His heart is not disgust or disappointment, but compassion, mercy, love, and excitement as he begins to sprint toward the son!

What rises up in the father's heart is not disgust or disappointment, but compassion, mercy, love, and excitement as he begins to sprint toward the son!

"and felt compassion for him, and ran and embraced him, and kissed him." (20c)

Jesus is painting a very specific visual here. In those days dignified landowners did not run, they walked with dignity. It's possible that the lack of running was due to the fact that they were essentially wearing dresses and flip flops, which made it challenging to maintain dignity while running in such a getup. At any rate, the picture to take away is one of a father so overwhelmed with love and compassion that he picks up his skirts and runs full barrel toward the son with his sandals flailing behind him. Can you see it? Now see the son, the cloud of filth surrounding him, his slow, tired movement barely advancing him forward, and the father creating a pillow of dust himself as he runs full speed toward him. Picture the moment when the father throws his arms wide open to embrace his lost son!

I imagine that the father could smell him from several meters away and yet he kept on coming without hesitation! Sometimes I wish the

Bible was "scratch and sniff." I think we would have a much more accurate understanding of what we read with that feature added. But back to the father and son, who are locked in an embrace, with the son's filth and stench getting all over the father, and yet He doesn't let go. In fact, the literal translation says the father "fell on the prodigal's neck." Do we imagine that is how the Father greets us upon our return, no matter how long the trip away? Do we think He embraces us as we are or do we think he needs us cleaned up first to be lovable? Jesus is giving us an illustration of a love that stops for nothing. Not stinking sin, not smelly shame, and not previous insults or woundings. The final segment of this verse says that the father kisses the son. Kissing was a sign of covenant, commitment, and belonging. The Father is saying clearly with his actions, "Welcome home, son, you are mine and I receive you unconditionally."

REFLECTION AND ACTIVATION

1. Reflect on how you expect the Father to greet you when you have messed up. Let's ask this today:

   "Daddy what do you want me to know about how You see me even when I make mistakes?"

2. Spend some time soaking and ask Him to reveal His heart for you even in the moments when you think He must have been the most disappointed. Journal your insights.

The Scripture says that the father kissed the son. The father is saying clearly with his actions, "Welcome home, son, you are mine and I receive you unconditionally."

Journal Notes

THE ANSWER IS IN THE ACTION

Lesson Notes

Yesterday we looked at the powerful imagery of the return of the prodigal son. We read about how the son headed home and encountered his father's heart that was so full of love and yearning that he broke with the custom of that day and ran out to meet him. In reading through this passage and combining that with the way I had always perceived God, I kept expecting somewhere in there, maybe after the embrace or the kiss, that the father would present this son with a contract of some sort – something that contains a repayment plan for all the money he squandered, or something that outlined what he would have to do to earn his way back into the father's heart and home. But, there is nothing like that in this passage because there is nothing like that in God's heart. His heart toward us is simply for us to return fully, to know we are loved wholly, and to be able to rest in that knowledge. So, let's pick up where we left off.

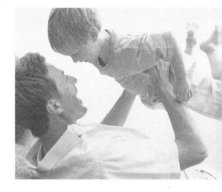

God's heart toward us is simply for us to return fully, to know we are loved wholly, and to be able to rest in that knowledge.

> *"And the son said to him, 'Father, I have sinned against heaven and in your sight; I am no longer worthy to be called your son.'" (Luke 15:21)*

I love it that the son launches into this speech. His dad has just run up to meet him but the son is still trying to sell him on being able to return. He is so focused on his failure that he cannot see the father's response and joy at his return. Mind you, it is a shame not to give a good speech, especially when you went to the trouble of practicing. I can almost see the father's face while the son is speaking – him smiling at the son with eyes of love that say, "Oh son, you just don't get it do you?"

"But the father said to his slaves, Quickly bring out the best robe and put it on him, and put a ring on his hand and sandals on his feet; And bring the fattened calf, kill it, and let us eat and be merry; For this son of mine was dead, and has come to life again; he was lost, and has been found. And they began to be merry." (Luke 15:22-24)

Now we see the father answer every facet of the son's negative expectations with actions not words. The first of these actions is this…

"Quickly bring out the best robe and put it on him" (22a)

Who do you think the best robe would have belonged to? Most likely it was the father's robe. In this passage the father answers some underlying issues that we all often face. This first issue is one of shame. Let's go back to that picture of the son upon his return for a moment. I would imagine his clothing would be in pretty rough shape from hanging out with pigs and walking all that way. I am sure he looked far from presentable and most likely he felt quite self-conscious before the household. Yet, the father answers the issue of shame not with, "This humiliation is what you deserve," but with his very own best robe, to cover his son's shame. The father also "put a ring on his hand and sandals on his feet" according to verse 22b.

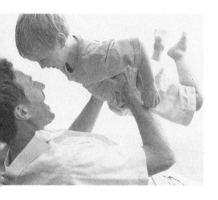

The father answers the issue of shame with his very own best robe to cover his son's shame.

These were both very significant gifts with very significant messages to the son's heart. In those days, giving him a ring would have been similar to giving him the family VISA card today. With his father's ring, he could go into town and buy things, with the ring serving as a token of the power of his father's ability to pay. This son has failed miserably with finances, and his father gives him a ring? Yes! What about you? What do you think God does with your financial failures? Can you bring them to Him and ask for help and mercy, or do you think you deserve the consequences of your actions and refuse to accept or receive mercy?

The next gift, the sandals, is equally as powerful, and says one thing: "You are my son." All of his issues with regard to belonging and sonship are answered in this demonstration. You see, slaves went barefoot but sons wore sandals. With all three gifts he is saying the same message: "You are my son, you are my son, you are my son." It is not about his performance, it never was! In fact, if God cared only for your performance we would have a very different and sad story being told here. But, He doesn't. He demonstrates his love and acceptance of the son without precondition and then he goes a step further. He celebrates the son.

The father throws a generous welcome home party with his heart so full of love it was as though he'd sent the son out to do his bidding and he returned having successfully done so. No mention of his squandering, no recollection of a father's broken heart, just a party to show off this son to his household and neighborhood friends. Listen, if someone told you God is not into parties they were wrong. They throw plenty of parties in heaven and He loves to celebrate! He parties over you as well.

REFLECTION AND ACTIVATION

Let's start with some soaking today and when you are finished soaking in the truth that He loves you with imperfections and all, then grab your journal and ask him the following:

1. Father, what is my heart expectation when I make mistakes? What do You want me to know about how You feel about me in those moments?

2. Papa, is there any shame that I am still hanging onto instead of taking your robe?

It is not about the son's performance, it never was! He demonstrates his love and acceptance of the son without precondition and then he goes a step further. He celebrates the son.

Journal Notes

THE OLDER SON

Lesson Notes

"Now his older son was in the field, and when he came and approached the house, he heard music and dancing. And he summoned one of the servants and began inquiring what these things might be.

"And he said to him, 'Your brother has come, and your father has killed the fattened calf, because he has received him back safe and sound.' But he became angry, and was not willing to go in; and his father came out and began entreating him. But he answered and said to his father, 'Look! For so many years I have been serving you, and I have never neglected a command of yours; and yet you have never given me a kid, that I might be merry with my friends; But when this son of yours came, who has devoured your wealth with harlots, you killed the fattened calf for him.'"

(Luke 15:25-30)

It is a feast with music and dancing and it was loud enough to be heard from a distance! The celebration was for the son who had returned home.

The context of this portion is that there is a party going on. It is a feast with music and dancing and it was loud enough to be heard from a distance! The celebration was for the son who had returned home.

What does your heart do when you see God celebrating someone that you know is far from perfect? When others are getting all the attention but you have been diligent to keep all the rules? How do you respond when all your effort seems meaningless because someone else was rewarded? Maybe your reaction would be similar to that of the older son in this story.

He had been working diligently out in the fields and upon his return from a hard day, he was greeted with the sound of rejoicing. I am sure he was wondering what was worthy of such a celebration. Upon inquiring he is told of his younger brother's return. I imagine the older son saw red that day! I mean seriously; this celebration is for HIM?!?!? I can understand him not wanting to go in and celebrate. He was probably counting to ten slowly in order to reign in his emotions – however, he was likely counting to 50 just to be sure! Let's pick it up here…

"But he became angry, and was not willing to go in; and his father came out and began entreating him." (Luke 15:28)

I love this verse as it gives us another little key into God's responses to us. He is not threatened by your anger. Even in the midst of it He can and will meet you right there and help you head in the direction of love. The father came right to where he was (physically and emotionally) to coach him to a healthy perspective.

The Father is not threatened by your anger. Even in the midst of it He can and will meet you right there and help you head in the direction of love.

"But he answered and said to his father, 'Look! For so many years I have been serving you, and I have never neglected a command of yours; and yet you have never given me a kid, that I might be merry with my friends; But when this son of yours came, who has devoured your wealth with harlots, you killed the fattened calf for him.'" (Luke 15:29,30)

You can almost hear the barely concealed outrage, can't you? "Hey, wait a minute, that's not FAIR! I've worked so hard for you and here comes trouble and you honor him!" The older son even goes so far as to call him, "this son of yours," as though he refuses to claim any family ties with him. The elder son is extremely angry and hurt, but only because he doesn't understand the heart of the father.

He responds in this manner because his mindset is about earning; therefore, the younger son doesn't deserve being celebrated, which, from that perspective, is correct. However, that is not the father's perspective; you could never earn the kind of love he extends in the first place, and that is where the older son misses the point.

How about you? What does your heart do when you see God celebrating someone that you know is far from perfect? What is your heart's reaction when they are getting all the attention but you have been diligent to keep all the rules and behave yourself?

REFLECTION AND ACTIVATION

1. Why don't you journal about any hurtful feelings you experienced when someone got celebrated with undeserved favor after they had made mistakes, while you did not feel celebrated for keeping the rules and behaving yourself? Ask Papa to reveal any area in your life that is still screaming, "It's not fair!"

2. Ask Holy Spirit to coach you through this. Invite Him to speak to your heart. What is He saying? Journal.

When you are finished journaling, grab your music and pillow again and rest in His love. Ask Him to wash away any ungodly drive to earn and strive for favor. Ask Him to teach you how to rest.

Journal Notes

_____

_____

_____

_____

_____

_____

_____

_____

_____

_____

_____

_____

_____

_____

_____

_____

WHICH ONE ARE YOU?

Lesson Notes

Jesus made a way home for us that is covered by grace and mercy, and powered by love.

As we finish the story of the "Prodigal Sons" today, let's invite the Holy Spirit to examine our hearts and lives for any internal demands for fairness. God isn't motivated by fairness, He is motivated by love. That is where the older son missed the point (and often we do, as well). The Old Testament comes from the perspective of fairness and performance, but Jesus made a way home for us that is covered by grace and mercy, and powered by love.

And he said to him, "Son, you have always been with me, and all that is mine is yours. 'But we had to be merry and rejoice, for this brother of yours was dead and has begun to live, and was lost and has been found.'" (Luke 15:31,32)

The Father's heart always goes after restoration – for the prodigals to turn their hearts toward home as they hear the call of love. But returning prodigals shouldn't make the other children feel less valuable or of more value. God is not short on love just like He is not short on finances, dreams, or words of encouragement. He is not facing a drought of love whereby He must conserve it only for those who feel they truly earned it. You cannot earn extravagant love, that's what makes it extravagant! Yes, I see you sitting in the second row, always on time and always serving, which is amazing and we celebrate you. Do you know that ALL that God has is yours? Yes, even on the days you don't "perform" well, all He has is still yours if you are a son. The tricky bit is making a transition in our hearts and mindsets from slave to son. We are going to spend the next two weeks focusing on that task.

In looking at the story from the perspectives of both sons, we can be sure of one thing: neither of them knew the heart of their father completely or how much he loved them. We know this because one of them felt degraded because of his guilt and shame, and the other was living like a slave, instead of a son in his house. He was striving to earn everything he received. Often in the church, we find ourselves in one of those two camps… self-degraded or slaving, but rarely resting and knowing we are loved.

REFLECTION AND ACTIVATION

1. Ask Daddy to reveal to you the areas you are still attempting to strive in or earn acceptance. Journal your thoughts as He speaks to you.

2. Ask Daddy to reveal to you areas of your life where you are self-degraded due to guilt and shame like the younger son. Are there areas where you are running away from Him rather than running to Him?

3. Are there any areas where you have given up altogether on sonship/daughtership like the younger son? Journal your thoughts.

Neither of them knew the heart of their father completely or how much he loved them.

4. Do you react like the older son when individuals are celebrated that you feel are not deserving of it?

5. Spend as long as you can soaking in Papa's love.

Journal Notes

ORPHAN THINKING

I would like to begin our study by giving credit where credit is due. Most of this teaching comes from the revelation of two truly gifted teachers regarding the Father's heart; their names are James Jordan and Jack Frost. I will be listing some of their teaching materials and where to get them in the resource section at the back of this study.

If you opened your Bible and begin reading from John 14 through chapter 17, you would be reading Jesus' final conversation with the disciples before going to the cross. In these chapters are several verses we have already explored in the course of our study together. One verse, however, seems to come right out of nowhere. Jesus explains that He is "the way" to the Father and then goes on to describe the role of the Holy Spirit; right in the middle of that description is this statement:

"I will not leave you as orphans; I will come to you." (John 14:18 ESV)

Jesus summarizes God's Father heart toward His people by saying "I will not leave you as orphans."

It seems fairly random, at least in its placement, but we know that Jesus only said what He heard the Father saying. Here, in the middle of preparing the disciples to be without Him and telling them about the Holy Spirit, Jesus summarizes God's Father heart toward His people: I will not leave you as orphans; I will come to you. It is the promise of the third person of the Trinity being with them and not leaving them to fend for themselves, but it brings to mind some interesting questions! What exactly made these men orphans? Was it just a statement of circumstance? Were they all without fathers? We know who some of the disciples' fathers were, so Jesus must be addressing something else. Perhaps He was referring to a spiritual state or a way of living or thinking - a mindset, if you will.

So what is an orphan in this context? Simply put, an orphan is someone who lives outside of the Father's presence. The atmosphere of heaven is one of continuous love twenty-four hours a day, seven days a week. Therefore, an orphan is someone who lives outside of that love more than they live in it. I honestly think the best definition of hell is being away from the Father you were created to be loved by eternally.

Let's skip back to the beginning; to Genesis and have a look at how it all began…

The LORD God formed the man from the dust of the ground and breathed into his nostrils the breath of life, and the man became a living being. (Genesis 2:7)

James Jordan made such an interesting observation about this verse. He said, "I wonder if it looked to the angels like God was kissing Adam." I mean, you have to get pretty close to someone to breathe into their nostrils. Now imagine the very first thing that Adam would have seen as he opened his eyes after this first breath – he would have seen the very eyes of Love Himself. In that moment Adam knew no insecurity or failure, no anger or regret - he simply knew love. He was face to face with pure love, the kind of love that is life to every part of you. You and I were created to experience His love like that, face to face with Him before sin came into the world.

But sin did come into the world, and in that next conversation when the Lord begins talking to them about what has happened we see this …

Then the LORD God said to the woman, "What is this you have done?"
The woman said, "The serpent deceived me, and I ate." (Genesis 3:13)

Right from the very beginning as soon as sin appears on the scene, we can see Adam and Eve blame shifting as fast as they can. They had already learned to hide their shame in excuses.

Adam named his wife Eve… (Genesis 3:20 NIV)

Before this time (vs. 20) they were Adam together, but after sin enters the picture so does separation between the sexes with striving, division and animosity. We were created to live as one together, but the orphan spirit is now on the rise and it brings with it a divisive, and competitive mindset.

An orphan is someone who lives outside of the Father's presence.

And the LORD God made garments of skin for Adam and his wife, and clothed them. (Genesis 3:21)

Again, I love God's heart in this. It was never His desire that they would know they were naked, or that they would experience shame so He makes clothes for them and covers them.

Then the LORD God said, "Behold, the man has become like one of Us, knowing good and evil; and now, he might stretch out his hand, and take also from the tree of life, and eat, and live forever" —

Therefore the LORD God sent him out from the garden of Eden, to cultivate the ground from which he was taken. So He drove the man out; and at the east of the garden of Eden He stationed the cherubim, and the flaming sword which turned every direction, to guard the way to the tree of life. (Genesis 3:22-24)

The final verses of chapter three can seem difficult to understand in the context of a loving God. It doesn't seem very loving of God to kick his children out of the garden to cultivate dry lands. But what I missed in this was God's reasoning and his Father's heart. If He had allowed them to stay and they had eaten of the tree of life, it would have been devastating! They would have lived forever morally disintegrating and how could a loving Father watch that? No, He needed to implement a plan to restore us, but He couldn't allow it to get worse by allowing Adam and Eve to live forever.

I cannot imagine how it must have hurt God's heart to drive them from the garden. He had created them for relationship; to love them and be loved by them, and now everything had gone horribly wrong. The Father's cry from that moment on echoes throughout Scripture, as He sent prophets, judges, kings and even talking animals to turn the people back to Him – all declaring His heart, "I will not leave you as orphans; I will come to you." Finally, Jesus came to be "the way" home.

His disciples had been walking with Him for three years and were still behaving like orphans. Even today, we find many in the church who know Jesus still living and behaving like orphans.

> The Father's cry echoes throughout Scripture, as He sent prophets, judges, kings and even talking animals to turn the people back to Him – all declaring His heart, "I will not leave you as orphans; I will come to you."

Therefore, our next question is: how does an orphan behave? They have to fight for everything they feel they need, and they cannot rest. They do not find Father God to be a haven of safety or a shelter to run into. They have no sense of belonging and they have no feeling of significance or expectation of inheritance.

A son or daughter on the other hand, knows he/she is an heir and that there is a safe place in the Father's lap. Sons and daughters believe that they are fully loved and they are able to rest in that.

Jack Frost defines an orphan in this way: "The orphan spirit causes one to live life as if he does not have a safe and secure place in the Father's heart. He feels he has no place of affirmation, protection, comfort, belonging, or affection. Self-oriented, lonely, and inwardly isolated, he has no one from whom to draw godly inheritance. Therefore, he has to strive, achieve, compete, and earn everything he gets in life. It easily leads to a life of anxiety, fears, and frustration."

The spirit of Sonship is about security, significance, identity, patience, basic trust, faithfulness, loyalty, humility, and being others-oriented. The orphan spirit or mindset is one of slavery to fear, rejection and insecurity, and Father God doesn't want us living like that anymore.

Sons and daughters believe that they are fully loved and they are able to rest in that knowledge.

For the remainder of this study we are going to work through a chart that Jack Frost developed that we'll use as a diagnostic tool to discover areas where we are still behaving like orphans. The first time I saw this chart, I was shocked to find that many of my responses to situations and to God were almost entirely orphan reactions. Yet, when I heard the teaching again many months later, I realized there had been a real shift in my mindset toward sonship/daughtership. There were certainly still areas of struggle, but as I invited God to reveal my place in His heart as a daughter and not an orphan, I was encouraged to see He was doing just that. I know He will be just as faithful to you if you will allow Him to help you look at your heart motivations and reactions, and bring healing and restoration of trust in Him to your heart.

CHART OF DOOM

Lesson Notes

Over the next two weeks we are going to be walking through the diagnostic chart I mentioned in this week's introduction. Each day we will look at a few different challenges, thoughts, or circumstances and examine how an orphan reacts as opposed to how a son or daughter responds.

Image of God

- The orphan sees God as a master.

- The son/daughter, knows God as a loving Father.

If we believe God is a loving Father, we will introduce others to a loving relationship with Him.

These opposing viewpoints will make a huge difference in a number of areas. If we think God is a Master, then our walk with Him becomes about a list of what we do and do not do. We constantly need to perform and work for Him and we cannot rest. Yet if we know him as a loving Father, we will relate and serve out of a completely different place. We know we are loved and because we are, we enjoy partnering with Him and being with Him. We are His beloved children, not His employees, and as such, we are free to have a close relationship with Him.

If we believe through an orphan mentality that God is a Master, then when we lead someone to the Lord, we will bring them home to a set of rules. If we believe He is a loving Father, we will introduce them to a loving relationship with Him.

Theology

- The orphan lives by the love of the Law.

- The son/daughter lives by the law of love.

The orphan mentality is about a list of things you can and cannot do. Orphans need the list so they can judge themselves and others with a clear set of guidelines and feel righteous about the verdict it renders. When you choose to live by the law, you don't need to hear God's voice or have a two- way relationship because it's all in the law; just do it.

The son and daughter however, live by the law of love, extending grace to others and therefore continuously receiving grace for themselves. Their internal compass is set to what the Love of God desires in any situation.

Personally, I was an orphan in both of the areas of my image of God and my theological perspective. I totally viewed God as a Master, which of course doesn't make Him someone you want to get close to even if you thought it was possible. The first four years of my walk with God was almost entirely about the list with a mentality of, "Just tell me what I can do and what I can't do." I had no idea God would speak to me as His daughter or desired a genuine loving relationship. My adjusted and renewed perspective has been a really nice change!

A son or daughter will live by the law of love, extending grace to others and therefore continuously receiving grace for themselves.

REFLECTION AND ACTIVATION

1. Have a little chat with God about these two areas of perspective. Ask Him to show you how you see Him. Examine how you respond to love and law.

2. If you are the kind of person who likes to chart things and be able to look back and see what God has done, then I would suggest for each of these areas you draw a line and number it from 1 to 10, with 1 being fully orphan understanding in this area and 10 being fully living as a son/daughter in this area.

   Then ask the Father where your current understanding is for each area. In a few months if you look back and ask the Father the same thing, you will likely find you have moved up higher into sonship/daughtership! Your chart may look something like this:

Image of God

1	2	3	4	5	6	7	8	9	10

Theology

1	2	3	4	5	6	7	8	9	10

3. Now go ahead and just soak in His love for as long as you can!

Journal Notes

_____

_____

_____

_____

_____

_____

_____

_____

_____

_____

_____

_____

_____

_____

_____

_____

_____

_____

MORE CHART OF DOOM

The son or daughter enjoys their full acceptance and justification in God's love and grace.

Lesson Notes

We are still working through what Alyn and I call the "Chart of Doom!" While we travelled for many years we would often teach on the orphan spirit and go through this chart. The first time through, most discover that they behave like orphans (we sure did), which is why we affectionately call this chart the "Chart of Doom." While we were teaching we would encourage the group to make the scary "Oooo" sound each time we say "Chart of Doom." You should try this too when you fill out your charts!

It is helpful to understand that just because you have some orphan tendencies or moments, it doesn't mean you behave and respond to God and others like an orphan all the time! We call it "orphaning out" when the orphan thoughts soar to the surface to make their presence felt!

Don't be discouraged when orphan behaviors still pop up. The good news is that when you go through this chart regularly, you can catch it quicker, and identify it when it is still a thought (in other words, before it comes flying out of your mouth!). The more you identify and adjust the behavior, the less you will respond with orphan tendencies. Be patient and continue to move forward.

Dependency

- The orphan is independent and self-reliant.

- The son/daughter is interdependent and acknowledges need in a healthy way.

Galatians 6:2 encourages us to bear one another's burdens. If we are living like orphans we can't accomplish this because we are an island unto ourselves. Orphans don't need, or more to the point, don't want to need other people for anything. Sons and daughters, on the other hand, can both ask for and allow others to help them. They do not see needing help as making them less of a person but simply view helping and being helped as what family does for each other.

Security

- The orphan is insecure and lacks peace.

- The son/daughter is at rest and abides in peace.

How are you at resting? For me it is something I have learned to do over a number of years. My inability to rest stemmed from the insecurity of "what will people think." The orphan can't rest because he/she is insecure like I was (and still am in moments of "orphaning out"). The orphan can't find that place of peace and just relax. Soaking for the orphan heart is exceptionally difficult.

Need for Approval

- The orphan strives for the praise, approval, and acceptance of others.

- The son or daughter enjoys their full acceptance and justification in God's love and grace.

Ouch! This one stings a bit doesn't it? Striving for approval was a way of life for me due to all my performance issues before I even met the Lord. I needed someone to notice me and praise me for all the things I was trying to do. I was wounded if my contributions were not recognized when others' were. When we are finally able to live from the place of knowing we are loved and accepted by God, we can rest in a job well done without worrying about obtaining the credit for it.

Orphans don't need, or more to the point, don't want to need other people for anything. Sons and daughters, on the other hand, can both ask for and allow others to help them.

REFLECTION AND ACTIVATION

1. Again, let's take some time to allow the Holy Spirit to enlighten us with the three areas we have covered today.

    Just ask Him where you are on each little scale.

Dependency

1	2	3	4	5	6	7	8	9	10

Security

1	2	3	4	5	6	7	8	9	10

Need for approval

1	2	3	4	5	6	7	8	9	10

2. Now grab your journal and ask Papa these questions:

    a. Have You been asking me to learn to rest in you? What still stands in the way of me learning to rest?

    b. When my insecurities flare up, what do You want me to know about how You feel about me?

    c   Do You love and accept me?

    d. Do I live like You do?

3. Now spend the remainder of your time soaking and taking in His love.

When we live from the place of knowing we are loved and accepted by God, we can rest in a job well done without worrying about obtaining the credit for it.

Journal Notes

CHART OF DOOM continued...

Lesson Notes

More from the "chart of doom"... (Did you say "Oooo" in your heads?)

Motive for Service

Sons and daughters serve because it's their joy to do so.

- The orphan needs personal achievement in order to impress God and others. In some cases there is no motivation to serve at all.

- The son or daughter's service is motivated by a deep gratitude for being unconditionally loved and accepted by God.

I don't know if you have noticed, but a funny thing happens when we start coming to church... we bring all our unresolved issues with us! If we are from performance-oriented homes, we often attach those perspectives onto God, church, and the pastors in the area of service. We volunteer for anything that might get us in the path or sight of the person we seek to impress.

I am certainly not saying that service is bad; just the opposite. In fact, service is necessary and holy unto God, but what we are examining is the motivation behind it. Sons and daughters serve because it's their joy to do so. They take ownership in the areas they serve in and they serve well without needing to be seen or commended. John Arnott says lovers and sons will out-perform orphans or strivers ten to one.

Motive Behind Christian Disciplines

- The orphan's motive is performing duty in order to earn God's favor or no motivation at all.

- The son/daughter's motive is pleasure and delight.

You may have noticed the phrase "or no motivation at all" in the previous two areas we looked at, but let's elaborate on how that manifests. We look at our lives and say, "Well, I don't strive, need approval, or try to earn God's favor, so I'm good, thanks." But often, this is because we have given up, and are speaking from a position of brokenness. That's the "no motivation at all," we've been speaking about. We often shut down and therefore don't attempt to try in any area we have previously disappointed ourselves. We conclude that this is how we avoid the pain of failing.

In disciplines such as spending time with God, the orphan mindset either gives up, performs to earn His favor, or punches some sort of celestial time clock.

Sons and daughters are disciplined about pursuing and responding to God's voice because they know they are loved, so it's all a pleasure. There is so much freedom in that! As a result of that secure position, on those days that they don't manage to spend personal time with God they know they are still loved. In fact, they want to make sure they meet with Him the next day simply because they miss Him.

Sons and daughters are disciplined about pursuing and responding to God's voice because they know they are loved.

Motive for Purity

- The orphan "must" be holy to have God's favor, thus increasing a sense of shame and guilt.

- The son or daughter "wants" to be holy and does not desire anything to hinder intimate relationship with God.

This mindset for the orphan will again keep him/her in a place of striving and then failing, striving and failing, which is a very frustrating cycle. Eventually the orphan may stop trying for purity as it's all powered by self-effort and it is exhausting to continue the effort.

Out of love for the Lord, the son or daughter wants to be holy and can lean on God for help. They are able to receive that help from others and stay accountable because their relationship with the Lord is a priority.

REFLECTION AND ACTIVATION

1. By now you know the drill! Here are the scales for you to ask the Holy Spirit to speak into and then we will ask the Lord some questions.

Motive for Service

1	2	3	4	5	6	7	8	9	10

Motive Behind Christian Disciplines

1	2	3	4	5	6	7	8	9	10

Motive for Purity

1	2	3	4	5	6	7	8	9	10

Out of love for the Lord, the son or daughter wants to be holy and can lean on God for help.

2. Now let's journal and ask God these questions:

   a. Lord, in what areas am I striving for Your attention or trying to impress You?

   b. Are there any areas in which I have given up?

3. It's soaking time… spend as long as you can resting in His presence and allow His spirit of adoption to flow through you.

Journal Notes

YES, EVEN MORE OF THE CHART OF DOOM!

Lesson Notes

Rest in God's Presence and let His love minister to your heart.

How are you doing? Are you hanging in there? I know sometimes looking at this kind of stuff and letting God take a fine-toothed comb to your life is exhausting. But when you let God lead it and do the work of bringing issues to the surface, the healing is always amazing.

Self Image

- The orphan operates in self-rejection as a result of comparing themselves to others.

- The son or daughter is positive and affirming because they know they have great value to God.

This was a huge one with me and I am still in process. I love it that sons and daughters are not critical of themselves because they know they are fearfully and wonderfully made. They are loved, and they are valuable. Most of us grow up comparing ourselves to others from a very young age. We compare our grades at school, sports performance, weight, body shape and then later on in life our jobs, cars and houses all define how good or badly we feel about ourselves. Each time we come across someone who seems more successful, more beautiful or more fulfilled, our hearts sink a little bit more. That sinking is simply an orphan not knowing he is as loved and affirmed as he is at this very moment.

Source of Comfort

- The orphan seeks comfort in counterfeit affections such as: addictions, compulsions, escapism, busyness, and hyper-religious activity.

- The son or daughter seeks comfort through quietness and solitude, in order to rest in the Father's presence and love.

When everything in your life hits the fan, what does your heart do? When a major repair bill comes in, or a family member is diagnosed with a sickness, where do you run? For me, books and movies were my escape. When things were not going well, I would always read a book or go to the movies to run away from the reality of my life. At one point in time, I was ripping through 400-page novels in a day-and-a-half and I needed to have bought the next one ahead of time, or life might actually come back to the forefront of my mind. Others can hide in alcohol, work, volunteering for every possible position, eating, pornography, masturbation or maybe even sleep. Anything that we use to numb the pain instead of climbing up in Daddy's lap is likely to be a counterfeit affection.

The way of the son or daughter, while not producing that numbing effect that we may really want, is actually much better in the long run. Rest in God's presence and let His love calm your racing thoughts and heart. Listen for what He is trying to tell you. Whatever the news, whatever the situation, He has not lost sight of you! He has Holy Spirit GPS on your exact location and the circumstances you face, and He will not leave you nor forsake you in the midst of this.

Sons and daughters are not critical of themselves because they know they are fearfully and wonderfully made.

REFLECTION AND ACTIVATION

1. Take a few minutes and assess with God where things are at with these two areas:

Self-image

1	2	3	4	5	6	7	8	9	10

Source of Comfort

1	2	3	4	5	6	7	8	9	10

2. Here are today's questions:

   a. Daddy, in what areas do I still compare myself to others?

   b. What do You want to say about that?

   c. What do I run to when things get rough?

3. Soaking time! Hurray… grab your pillow and just rest in Him.

Journal Notes

_____

_____

_____

_____

_____

_____

_____

_____

_____

_____

_____

_____

_____

_____

_____

_____

_____

_____

_____

_____

HELLO CHART – I'VE MISSED YOU!

Lesson Notes

Do you feel like you are running a bit of an issue marathon? It really will be okay! We are going to look at the last two topics on the chart for this week and then you have a breather until we finish the rest of the chart in Week Eight.

Peer Relationships

A son or daughter values others and is able to rejoice in their blessings and successes.

- The orphan is competitive, and often engages in rivalry and jealousy toward others' successes and positions.

- The son or daughter is humble and walks in unity with others. They value others and are able to rejoice in their blessings and successes.

In Luke 9:46 we see the orphan spirit among the disciples – "And an argument arose among them as to which of them might be the greatest." It's comforting to know that even the disciples, who lived with Jesus, saw Him in action and learned from Him daily, still "orphaned out." They missed the point of Jesus' teaching and were caught up in competition and rivalry. Similarly, in Mark 10, James and John are trying to carve out positions of influence and honor in heaven – in v41 it says that the other disciples began to feel indignant toward James and John when they found out what the brothers had done. I'm sure that's quite the understatement! We looked at the older brother earlier and

WEEK 7 - DAY 5

saw his orphaned heart – he couldn't rejoice in the blessing and restoration of his younger brother, but instead, was jealous of his father's affection toward him.

However, sons and daughters are secure in their Fathers' love. They know there is enough to go around. In fact, they are so secure, that they want their brothers and sisters to excel in all things – mostly because they know they won't be overlooked themselves. They understand that their Father is a good Father. They don't need to strive for affection and as a result are not in competition with their peers. What a different way to live!

Handling Others' Faults

- The orphan accuses and exposes in order to make themselves look good by making others look bad.

- The son or daughter covers with love and seeks to restore others in a spirit of love and gentleness.

Because the orphan feels like he/she has nobody looking out for them, they need to take advantage of every opportunity to look good. What better opportunity than through the failures of others? This, unfortunately, can happen in the most insidious manner. Even in our Christian culture, we find individuals putting others down with pious overtones and condescending attitudes. It's all too easy to put others down with religious subtleties such as, "Brothers, we need to pray for Bob. I know that he's struggling with a few personal matters right now. I don't want to gossip, but I think he has fallen back into…" and in just a few short moments we've lowered other people's estimation of Bob. We can even cloak our judgments as "discernment." As in, "I discern that Bob is struggling with lust." While Bob looks bad, the one propagating the gossip manages to look spiritual.

The son or daughter however, having an abundance of love, only wants to cover and protect, just as his Father would do. His heart reflects the heart of the Father.

Sons and daughters are secure in their Fathers' love. They understand that their Father is a good Father. They don't need to strive for affection and as a result are not in competition with their peers.

REFLECTION AND ACTIVATION

1. Take a few minutes and assess with God where things are in your heart with these two areas:

Peer Relationships

1	2	3	4	5	6	7	8	9	10

Handling Others' Faults

1	2	3	4	5	6	7	8	9	10

2. Here are today's questions:

    a. Father, please show me any areas where I need to repent with regard to my peer relationships – how have I misunderstood my brother's heart?

    b. Lord, please help me grant mercy to others who fall, so that I may be shown mercy in my time of need. Please reveal any person I have judged.

3. Now, grab your journal, soak and ask God to shift you to the "son/daughter" side of the chart.

The son or daughter covers with love and seeks to restore others in a spirit of love and gentleness.

Journal Notes

SONSHIP/DAUGHTERSHIP

Lesson Notes

As you may have already guessed, we are not yet done with the Chart of Doom (Oooo). While I am sure just going through the first half has given us plenty to work on with God, there is still more! But be encouraged! You are in a glorious process of knowing who you are as God's son or daughter. Your heart is learning new truths that will enable it to respond to your Heavenly Father and to life differently.

I had a dream a number of years ago when I was smack dab in the middle of trying to digest this whole orphan mindset. In the dream I saw Father God sitting in a large plush armchair looking very comfortable. He invited me to come and sit with Him but I just stared at Him. I noticed that there was another armchair beside His and He motioned for me to get in it. I was grid-locked, but with no idea why… I mean the instructions seemed clear.

Then He said, "AJ, you don't understand your place or value yet. You think that when you come to meet with Me, I should pull a dusty folding chair out of a back cupboard and set it up for you. But I deeply value you as My daughter and I always want you close to Me. Your armchair is always right next to Mine waiting for you." In the dream I walked up to my gorgeous big red armchair. I climbed in and sat very properly in the center toward the front with my legs hanging down, ankles crossed, and hands in my lap. "He is watching me and must know I am on best behavior," I thought.

You are in a glorious process of knowing who you are as God's son or daughter.

He then said, "Get comfortable, honey, you don't have to sit properly. Sit whichever way you like." I tried a number of positions in this massive chair, including feet up in the air resting against the back and head hanging down toward the floor, and finally settled on leaning over the arm toward His chair. He then leaned over the arm of His chair until we were nose to nose. He smiled and we proceeded to talk for ages.

Before I woke up He said, "Your chair is always here and I am always available. You have two places you can sit: in your own chair, or with Me in Mine." The dream kind of rocked me on the inside. I knew God was trying to get the message deeper within me. He was highlighting places in my heart that still did not recognize how much He loves me, and that I am a daughter with my own chair in His living room. Often in my times with Him after having that dream, I've revisited those chairs with Him. I go there still in my mind's eye and remind my heart of the truths I started learning years ago: I am His, I can always approach Him and He loves to see me; I am his daughter.

God said "Your chair is always here and I am always available."

OH, HELLO AGAIN, CHART!

Lesson Notes

Let's just jump right in…

View of Authority

- The orphan sees authority as a source of pain and lacks trust toward them. They find it difficult to embrace submission.

- The son/daughter is respectful and honoring toward authority. They view authority as ministers of God for good in their life.

If our experiences with authority figures have been painful or abusive, then we will have a great deal of difficulty trusting anyone that God has sent to help us grow or love. That applies to God as well, since He is the ultimate authority. As orphans we are not open to receive their counsel or input even if it is just from the pulpit on Sunday mornings. However, if we embrace the spirit of sonship/daughtership we can allow authority figures to give input and we can honor them as valuable for leading us into deeper relationship with Him.

I recognize in even broaching this subject that many of us have been very badly hurt by spiritual authority figures in the past. Some of these people may have manipulated you with words like "godly obedience and submission." I am certainly NOT suggesting that you blindly submit to anyone claiming authority. What I would encourage you to do is

> If we embrace the spirit of sonship/daughtership we can allow authority figures to give Input and we can honor them as valuable for leading us into deeper relationship with Him.

ask the Lord to supply to you or highlight to you the leaders He may have already provided that are safe. By safe I mean they themselves are under godly authority, and seek healing for the issues in their own lives. They don't lord things over people or try to appear perfect, but are genuine, approachable, godly and loving people with whom your heart feels safe. Leaders who have a track record of releasing sons and daughters of theirs into their destiny may still make some mistakes in leading, but the difference becomes that they can own them. That is the kind of leader you are looking for, and they are out there.

View of Admonition:

- The orphan has difficulty receiving healthy admonition. The orphan "must be right" so can easily get their feelings hurt and close their heart to the benefits of discipline.

- The son/daughter sees godly admonition as a blessing and knows it is needed in their life in order to expose and put to death faults and weaknesses.

What is admonition? By definition, it means to warn or reprimand, to advise or urge earnestly. Which of us likes to be disciplined by someone? Who wants to be sat down and set straight by someone who is supposed to love you? Ummm … sons and daughters do. When a son or daughter is warned or corrected by godly authority, they are able to recognize that it is a sign of love to care enough to correct them. It means that this person cares about me enough to help me stay on the right path toward all that God has for me. Let's look at this verse for a moment…

When a son or daughter is warned or corrected by godly authority, they are able to recognize that it is a sign of love to care enough to correct them.

> And you have forgotten the exhortation which is addressed to you as sons, "My son, do not regard lightly the discipline of the Lord, Nor faint when you are reproved by Him; For those whom the Lord loves He disciplines, And He scourges every son whom He receives.

> It is for discipline that you endure; God deals with you as with sons; for what son is there whom his father does not discipline? But if you are without discipline, of which all have become partakers, then you are illegitimate children and not sons.. (Hebrews 12:5-8)

We can see from this verse that discipline is to be equated with love but that is certainly not how I used to take it. I remember when I first started going to TACF and John and Carol Arnott would mention things that needed addressing in my life. On the outside I would maintain a smile and tell them I would pray about whatever it was that had concerned them, but on the inside I was furious that they had brought it up and was convinced they didn't love me and were judging me. Orphans don't like discipline and they don't receive it well, even if they really need it. I didn't have a healthy experience with discipline in the home growing up and therefore, I didn't know what to do with it as an adult. I encourage you to allow those people that God has brought around to parent you, to do their jobs and love you back to life. But know that the process will include discipline at times.

What if they are wrong? Well, what if they are? I remember John asking us permission to speak into our lives even if he later realized he got it wrong. We gave him permission because we knew if he did get it wrong he would be the first to come and apologize. Find safe, healed, humble leaders and let them help you become a son or daughter where you are.

REFLECTION AND APPLICATION

1. Take a few minutes and assess with God where things are at in these two areas:

View of Authority

1	2	3	4	5	6	7	8	9	10

View of Admonition

1	2	3	4	5	6	7	8	9	10

2. Here are some questions for you to journal about today:

    a. Daddy what is my heart response to admonition from others?

    b. Please highlight to me those that You have sent to help mold me and lead me and re-parent.

Find safe, healed, humble leaders and let them help you become a son or daughter.

3. Now grab a pillow and spend some time soaking in His Presence!

Journal Notes

_____

_____

_____

_____

_____

_____

_____

_____

_____

_____

_____

_____

_____

_____

_____

_____

_____

_____

_____

_____

_____

OH GOODY, MORE ISSUES…

Lesson Notes

Expression of Love

- The orphan is guarded and conditional in the way they express love. They base their release of love on the performance of others as they seek to get their own needs met. They are not free to love unconditionally.

- The son / daughter is open to love others, patient, and affectionate as they lay their lives and agendas down in order to meet the needs of others.

It's just flat out exhausting to be trapped in an orphan mindset. When you never know deep within that you are truly loved, life becomes all about survival. An orphan can only be friends or remain friends as long as everything goes their way. They are typically "fair weather friends" both with others and with God. As long as it looks like God is answering all their prayers with a "Yes," and things are going well, then they will maintain a great friendship with Him. But as soon as there is a delay in the answer, or things get difficult it becomes, "Where are you God? I tithe! I pray! I…" and the rant continues. Friendship, as long as you are getting your own way is not friendship at all. The orphan only stays friends with people as long as they make them look good, feel good, advance their agenda, and always comply without confrontation.

When you never know deep within that you are truly loved, life becomes all about survival.

The son or daughter, however, is able to lay down their life, time, and agenda for those who can give them nothing in return. They welcome confrontation when needed and are faithful and loyal.

Sense of God's Presence

- The orphan usually feels distant and can sometimes sense the loving presence of God when they feel they have met their self-appointed conditions.

- The son or daughter experiences close and intimate times with God.

The above definitions say it all. Where is God when everything falls apart or you have one of "those days"? Do you still feel Him near and know you are loved, or does He feel far away or angry with you? Do you walk around everyday and know that if you pause and listen He is right there; or do you have to earn His Presence with striving and effort?

Does God only feel close when you have completed your spiritual workout? Is His closeness and love for you based on your performance? What does your heart say when you feel like you have failed? Can you just crawl up in His lap and know that He is waiting for you?

REFLECTION AND ACTIVATION

The son or daughter is able to lay down their life, time, and agenda for those who can give him nothing in return.

1. Take a few minutes and assess with God where things are with these two areas:

Expression of Love

1	2	3	4	5	6	7	8	9	10

Sense of God's Presence

1	2	3	4	5	6	7	8	9	10

2. Let's journal and ask God these questions:

   a. Are there relationships in my life that are marked by this "fair weather friend" attitude on my part?

   b. What things send you into a place where you believe that you are on your own, God is distant, and you have failed again?

3. Take as long as you can today and carve out some time to soak and let His unconditional presence and love wash over you.

Journal Notes

_____

_____

_____

_____

_____

_____

_____

_____

_____

_____

_____

_____

_____

_____

_____

_____

_____

_____

_____

_____

YOU ARE ALMOST DONE!

Lesson Notes

Shall we count backwards from four? Yes, there are only four more areas to look at in our "Chart of Doom" and then we can just keep walking it out!

Condition

- The orphan lives in a state of bondage.

- The son/daughter lives in a state of liberty.

Sons and daughters are free to be themselves, free to be loved, and free to love others without restriction.

In bondage to what, you might ask? (Although I doubt at this point you are asking such a silly question!) But just in case, it could be fear, insecurity, fear of man, criticism, religiousness, fear of confrontation, needing to be right, competition, jealousy, vying for position and the list goes on. However, the son or daughter are free! They are free to be themselves, free to be loved, free to love others without restriction or criticalness, free from competition, free to rest, free to be childlike, and free to be all God called them to be without apology.

Vision

- The orphan's vision is usually full of spiritual ambition. They earnestly desire and strive for spiritual achievement. They long to be seen as mature and to be included in inner circles.

- The son/daughter's vision is to daily experience the Father's unconditional love and acceptance and then be sent as a representative of His love to others.

Have you ever been around the "green room" at a conference? There are those who are allowed in, and then those who are dying to be in there and striving to achieve the goal or entrance. Orphans need to be in there for at least one session so they can say, "Well, when I was in the green room with so and so and so and so..." Orphans will loiter around outside the door trying to catch eye contact with someone on the inside who might call them in, or they may make up excuses to need to just pass through.

Have you ever met, or been, the person who needs to be known by their title or who needs to drop their title into the conversation? Or what about the person who goes up to the speaker after the service with their own wisdom and Scripture verse, in order to impress the speaker - yep, they are an orphan too! Or how about the person who is networking and shaking hands during the service while everyone is trying to worship, yep you got it – orphan. Have you ever met that guy or girl? Have you ever been him/her? I have.

But the son or daughter is secure in the Father's love. They don't mind if they are invited into a green room or not. They are not offended if people don't remember them or if "important people" don't stop to chat. They can encourage others without having to say something impressive to feel good about the conversation. They don't need to name drop or weave in their resume or bring attention to who they have been with and where they have been. Sons and daughters are loved and they walk around with restful confidence because they know they are loved. They are full.

Sons and daughters are free to rest, free to be childlike, and free to be all God called them to be without apology.

REFLECTION AND ACTIVATION

1. Again, let's take a few minutes and assess with God where things are at with these two areas:

Condition

1	2	3	4	5	6	7	8	9	10

Vision

1   2   3   4   5   6   7   8   9   10

2. Now let's journal about these questions:

   a. Papa what areas of my heart are still in bondage?

   b. Papa, do I need to be seen and counted among the mature?

   c. Who do I "orphan out" around and need to impress?

3. Now try and spend at least 30 minutes soaking if you can and just invite Him to wash away the insecurities.

Journal Notes

_____

_____

_____

_____

_____

_____

_____

_____

_____

_____

_____

_____

_____

_____

_____

_____

_____

DNA

Lesson Notes

As we wrap up two weeks of looking at the "Chart of Doom" – and allowing the Holy Spirit to prompt us to recognize places where our fears and insecurities are robbing life from us, I think it would be great to look at some more Scriptures about sonship/daughtership.

For all who are being led by the Spirit of God, these are sons of God. For you have not received a spirit of slavery leading to fear again, but you have received a spirit of adoption as sons by which we cry out, "Abba! Father!" The Spirit Himself testifies with our spirit that we are children of God. (Romans 8:14-16)

You and I have received as believers the very DNA of God within us. The Holy Spirit comes as the spirit of adoption confirming to our hearts our status as sons and heirs. The Spirit testifies to this positional reality, that we are children of God. Whether we live like it yet or not we have received Him, received His DNA, and we are being transformed into the image of the Donor. It is the Holy Spirit within you that teaches your heart to cry out, "Abba! Daddy God!" He leads us away from living like slaves or servants and leads us to live like true sons and daughters.

The Holy Spirit testifies to the positional reality that we are children of God.

Let's look at one more area on the chart:

Position:

- The orphan feels like a slave or servant.

- The son/daughter feels like a beloved child.

There is no argument that stands against the knowledge and security of sonship/daughtership. As a true child of God you are free to be yourself because you know God will lead you, correct you, re-position you, envision you, and discipline you where needed so you are free! There is so much freedom in that kind of love and in the revelation of sonship/daughtership.

The orphans are still slaving away somewhere stuck in a cycle of striving and earning that they were not designed for. They are living a life with much less fullness then God designed and desired for them.

REFLECTION AND ACTIVATION

1. Ask the Holy Spirit to reveal to you how you are doing with this issue of sonship/daughtership. You might discover that you are already growing in this revelation.

Position

1	2	3	4	5	6	7	8	9	10

2. Let's journal a question or two:

   a. Daddy, am I living daily like I am Your son/daughter?

   b. In what circumstances do I still pull toward living like an orphan?

3. Spend time soaking in His Presence and invite Him to deepen the revelation of sonship/daughtership within you.

It is the Holy Spirit within you that teaches your heart to cry out "Abba! Daddy God!" He leads us away from living like slaves or servants and leads us to live like true sons and daughters.

Journal Notes

SONS AND DAUGHTERS IN THE HOUSE

When you are able to lay down your life and agenda and just serve someone for love's sake, then something changes.

Lesson Notes

I am a daughter of the house at the Toronto Airport Christian Fellowship as well as to John and Carol. That will never change no matter where I live or how long I am away. It can't be taken from me because I didn't grasp to have it or maintain it – it was given. We were woven together and we are entwined now.

I remember a number of years ago going up to the camp that TACF owned to spend a week writing in 2004. A friend had joined me to keep me company and get some rest as well. We settled into the cabin on Friday evening. A few hours later a man drove up the driveway and came up to the cabin. He thought he was staying there but had driven up to the wrong cabin. As he was leaving he turned around and we had the following conversation:

"Hey, aren't you John and Carol's daughter?"

I said, "No."

Then he said, "Yes, you are. I know you are."

I said, "No, I'm AJ."

He then said, "I knew I was right! You are their daughter!" as he got into his car.

I pondered that as he was leaving and said within myself, "Yes, I guess you are right."

Something changed at that point for me. I had a sense of belonging within and was able to embrace my "daughtership."

Later that week I had two more conversations with people that were absolutely convinced I was the Arnotts' child. I didn't start getting asked if I was their daughter until I started behaving like I was. I had spent years trying to allow myself to be parented while also trying to be independent and not appear to need help. The two don't work together well. But when you are able to lay down your life and agenda and just serve someone for love's sake, then something changes. It becomes your joy to see someone else succeed.

Jack Frost said submission is being "subject to another's mission." Sonship/daughtership isn't always about your mission, your vision or your dreams. At times, it's about the one who you are following and being a son or daughter to. True parents in the spirit live to see their children's visions and dreams realized. They will do whatever it takes to see maturity and fulfillment come to their sons and daughters. True sons and daughters on the other hand are happy and eager to serve the vision and mission of their leaders or spiritual fathers and mothers.

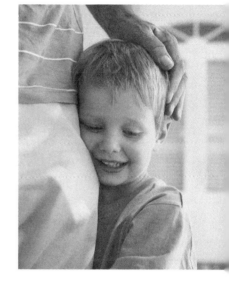

True parents in the spirit live to see their children's visions and dreams realized. They will do whatever it takes to see maturity and fulfillment come to their sons and daughters.

I encourage you to pray and ask God who the healed-up leaders and parents are that He has brought into your life to love and mold you; and then to find out where they feel called to go in God and help them get there. Be a son or daughter and get underneath whatever they are carrying and push up; help them get there without an eye on what you will get out of it. I promise you, sonship/daughtership releases inheritance! There are no crowbars required in the kingdom of heaven. God always sees and honors the faithful. Stop focusing on yourself and start focusing on being a son or daughter. Allow His blessings to overtake you.

The final area of the chart is this:

Future:

- The orphan fights for what they can get.

- The son/daughter lives in their bountiful inheritance.

I have been blessed beyond measure. In every area life has gone well with me once I truly began living like a daughter. I could not have opened all the doors that have been opened for us in these last eight years or so. But, I just determined in my heart to serve the leaders He sent me and they have propelled me forward and opened huge doors time after time.

The orphan, however, must fight, control, manipulate and strive to achieve the same things that are freely given to the son. I was listening to Larry Randolph one Sunday morning and he said something profound: "What you gain (position) by control, manipulation, or striving you will have to keep by control, manipulation and striving." That sums up the orphan; they are never satisfied. They never feel like they are where they are supposed to be because they manipulated their way in and need to continue to maintain it. The orphan can't just rest, serve someone else, and allow God to promote. Can you?

REFLECTION AND ACTIVATION

1. Well, you know what to do…..

Future

1	2	3	4	5	6	7	8	9	10

2. Let's journal and then soak today. Here are a few questions for you to get started:

   a. Holy Spirit whose son/daughter am I?

   b. Do I allow them to parent me, or am I still running in my heart from love and discipline?

   c. Whose vision are You asking me to get underneath and push up? How can I best do that?

   d. Have I been trying to gain position or favor by control, manipulation or striving?

3. Now just spend some time soaking and asking God to pour out the Spirit of sonship/daughtership over any orphan wounds that

God always sees and honors the faithful.

are surfacing. If you don't know who you are supposed to be a son or daughter to, then ask the Holy Spirit to tell you or send them. He will because He is so incredibly interested in you being parented, or re-parented properly!

Journal Notes

_____

_____

_____

_____

_____

_____

_____

_____

_____

_____

_____

_____

_____

_____

_____

_____

_____

_____

_____

_____

_____

PSALM 139

When I was first trying to get the message of the Father Heart of God established in my life, I spent an enormous amount of time in Psalm 139. I had it written on my mirrors at home on post-it notes, and read it almost daily. I needed it not only because it is jammed packed regarding His heart toward us, but also because there is a world of truth within it that is the antidote for a world of insecurity within us. Added to that, I just really appreciate David and the things he wrote. Scripture refers to David as a man after God's own heart, and I think part of the reason he became known as that was due to his honesty and vulnerability.

When you read through the Psalms you are never left wondering how David is feeling, what he is struggling with, and what he is longing for God to do in his situation. I actually think God likes that! No disguises, no pretence or hunger strikes (otherwise known as fasting to some), but just honesty. "God, this is how I feel and how the world looks to me, will You help?"

David was wild for God, abandoned, and yet far from perfect. God was kindly disposed toward him even in the midst of his imperfections because of his honesty.

The Psalms read like a chronicle or journal of David's relationship with God, and by them we know that David knew Him. David was wild for God, abandoned, and yet far from perfect. I believe God was kindly disposed toward him even in the midst of his imperfections because of his honesty. I know I have had seasons of trying to say only the "right things" to God; and then I have had seasons when I could only manage to say what was real without filters because I didn't have the strength to make it sound pretty. Upon reflection, it was during the raw moments that I really felt Him the closest. There were no masks, walls, or pretenses in those moments – it was just me in all my woundedness and Him in all His overwhelming love and grace for me.

We will look at Psalm 139 this week primarily in two versions: the NASB which has been the version I have read since meeting the Lord in 1986 and the Message, which often gives a different light to the passages as you read through. It also forces me to hear in a different way what He wants me to understand about each sentence.

Let's look at the opening in the Message and then the NASB:

GOD, investigate my life; get all the facts firsthand.

(Psalms 139:1 The Message)

O LORD, You have searched me and known me. (Psalms 139:1)

David's heart was to be known by God. He understood that God knew him – his weaknesses and his strengths, his challenges and his victories – and he invited God into the midst of his motivation and understanding.

My challenge to you this week as you read through this Psalm is to be as honest as David was about his thoughts, desires, and concerns, and hear what God wants to say to you.

David was as a man after God's own heart and became known throughout the Psalms as a man of honesty and vulnerability.

HE KNOWS YOU INSIDE OUT

Lesson Notes

GOD, investigate my life; get all the facts firsthand.

I'm an open book to You; even from a distance, You know what I'm thinking. You know when I leave and when I get back; I'm never out of Your sight. You know everything I'm going to say before I start the first sentence.

I look behind me and You're there, then up ahead and You're there, too— Your reassuring presence, coming and going. This is too much, too wonderful—I can't take it all in!   (Psalms 139:1 – 6 The Message)

God has searched you and He knows you. He knows your thoughts from afar and still chooses to come close.

Have you ever prayed prayers in your head and modified the wording of them on the fly to make it sound more spiritual or perhaps more palatable to the Lord? I have. I was never really taught to pray so I tried to pay attention every time we would be in those painful prayer circles where each person would pray out loud for something. I would hope against hope that no one would steal what I had thought to pray about before it got to my turn. I carefully crafted the prayer in my head and patiently waited for my turn to impress the circle with my spiritual wording and deep thoughtfulness. I think sometimes we try to do that with God. We don't want to be an open book! We are afraid of what kind of things would be found in those pages – our real thoughts, hurts, and the things that we are trying to hide from God and man.

Well, here is the thing… Your life IS an open book to Him whether you like it or not, so you might as well engage with the process. He knows what we are thinking at every moment and the amazing truth is that He still chooses to be near us!

Here's a scary thought for you: what if the thoughts of your mind were always printed on a screen above your head for the world to see – every critical thought or manipulative plan? Would you want it read? Well God can see all, and He still chooses you! That is amazing, isn't it? I know what passes through my head: critical thoughts about myself and others, unkind observations mixed with thoughts of wonder and joy at people's giftings and how they touch me. The whole gamut is right up there on the screen. It's scary, if you ask me, but it doesn't scare God at all.

He has searched you and He knows you. He knows your thoughts from afar and still chooses to come close. In fact, if you look at verse four it tells us that He even knows what we are going to say before we know it ourselves. Even when we have said things we wished we had never put into audible words, God knew before and He didn't back away from us. He simply waited for us to turn around and find Him right there waiting to love us back to life again. He lovingly washes the screens of our mind from everything that is not of Him. He is not intimidated when we are being transparent. He knows it already anyway, so why don't you start being real with Him and let Him breathe healing into the depths of your being?

GOD... You know when I leave and when I get back; I'm never out of Your sight.

Looking at verses three and five above, David also paints another familiar reality for us: you are not alone, not even for a moment. Father God has a Holy Spirit GPS on you. He knows when you leave and when you return and no matter how far or fast you run, you are never out of His sight. However, should you choose to run, He will be waiting for your return. That makes me think there isn't much point in running, and that perhaps surrender and honesty is the best path in moving forward.

I believe verse six is David's heart response to unconditional love. We don't naturally understand that kind of love but it is there, and that's how He loves us whether we can comprehend it or not.

Wow!

REFLECTION AND ACTIVATION

1. Take a few moments and reflect on today's verses. There are some truths our hearts need to know:

    *   He is not ashamed of you.

    *   He knows everything about you.

    *   He knows where you are and what you are doing every moment.

    *   He loves you.

2. How about soaking first today? Read over those first six verses again and then spend some time meditating on the truth while allowing God to wash over you.

3. Now let's grab our journals and ask God a few questions:

    a. Daddy when you investigate my life what do You see?

    b. Daddy when you investigate my heart what do You see?

    c. When was the last time I tried to run from You in my heart?

    d. What do You want me to know about that moment?

This is too much, too wonderful – I can't take it all in! (Psalms 139.6)

Journal Notes

HE IS EVERYWHERE…

Lesson Notes

Is there anyplace I can go to avoid Your Spirit? To be out of Your sight?

If I climb to the sky, You're there! If I go underground, You're there! If I flew on morning's wings to the far western horizon, You'd find me in a minute— You're already there waiting!

Then I said to myself, "Oh, He even sees me in the dark! At night I'm immersed in the light!" It's a fact: darkness isn't dark to You; night and day, darkness and light, they're all the same to You.

(Psalm 139: 7-12 The Message)

Even in the moments when we feel distant, He is right there. Whether we have spent time running or seem tired, weary and bogged down, He is still right there.

He really is everywhere, isn't He? I remember speaking at a church in Dallas, Texas, a number of years ago. In two days I had taught 12 sessions and I was utterly exhausted. I was so tired that I was sitting on my bed early Sunday morning after having breakfast with my hosts and wondering how on earth I was going to pull energy for speaking that morning. I said in my head, "Good Morning, Papa, it's me." And whoosh, the Holy Spirit landed on the bed and I was totally overwhelmed with His love. I said out loud, "Oh Papa, You found me!" and all I heard from Him was, "Sweetheart, I never lost you."

Even in the moments when we feel distant, He is right there. Whether we have spent time running like we talked about yesterday, or seem tired, weary and bogged down, He is still right there. Even in the darkest moments when we feel completely isolated or overwhelmed, God is with us..

The secret is training our hearts to turn to Him in those moments of exhaustion or absolute frustration, and let Him visit with us right where we are. He knows you, knows your thoughts, knows your struggles and challenges, knows your stress level and sleep issues and He wants to meet you in the midst of them – if you will let Him.

REFLECTION AND ACTIVATION

1. Let's begin with soaking again today. Invite the Holy Spirit to wash over you with the truth that you are never alone. Try to rest and receive His truth – you are never alone!

2. After soaking, grab your journal and invite Him to talk to you about a few things:

   a. Ask the Holy Spirit to remind you of the last time you felt alone or overwhelmed. In your mind's eye, ask Papa where He was that day and what He wants to tell you in regards to that moment.

   b. Papa where do I run in moments of desperation? What do You want to say about that?

He knows you, knows your thoughts, knows your struggles... and He wants to meet you in the midst of them – if you will let Him.

Journal Notes

_____

_____

_____

_____

_____

_____

_____

_____

_____

_____

_____

_____

_____

_____

_____

_____

_____

_____

_____

_____

_____

_____

_____

_____

_____

_____

_____

GOD HAS TINY FINGERS...

Lesson Notes

If you are here, and you are, then you are His plan. You were planned by God and born for such a time as this! You are NOT a mistake!

Oh yes, You shaped me first inside, then out; You formed me in my mother's womb. I thank You, High God—You're breathtaking! Body and soul, I am marvelously made! I worship in adoration—what a creation! (Psalm 139:13,14 The Message)

This Scripture is very clearly stating the following truth: "You were planned." You may have been a surprise to your parents, but you were no surprise to Him. The King of the universe, Father of all creation, He who made the stars, planets and solar systems has tiny fingers! He must, because He got right in there in your mother's womb and formed you!

People have funny ideas about getting pregnant and how easy or hard it is. Statistics show that even if both partners are very healthy, young and fit and are doing everything "right," they still have a one in five chance of getting pregnant. Then add to that the statistics on miscarriages and complications, and the truth is that YOU are an absolute miracle. With our first baby, Alyn and I tried for 10 months to conceive. We had the whole thing charted out and knew the "optimal time" for success according to experts, and it still took us 10 months to become pregnant. In between our two daughters I experienced two miscarriages. These experiences confirmed to my heart that there are no mistakes! If you are here, and you are, then you are His plan. You were planned by God and born for such a time as this! You are NOT a mistake!

He wove you together using your parents' DNA. He picked your eye color, hair color (even if you have messed with it) and the color of your skin; and then He said, "Perfect!"

Even though I know in my head that God wonderfully created me, I still feel free to criticize His handy work by being critical of myself. I have looked in the mirror and called ugly what God has called marvelous! I came to the conclusion several years ago that I wasn't going to be able to reason myself out of this one, but I actually needed to ask God for His eyes and His perspective when looking at me. And that's when things started to shift.

REFLECTION AND ACTIVATION

1. Let's journal first today and ask these questions:

   a. Daddy, am I calling anything ugly or un-valuable that You have called marvelous?

   b. Father, will You please tell me how You see me and give me Your eyes to see myself?

2. Okay, it's soaking time. Get comfortable and spend some time letting Him wash out all false perspectives about who You are, what You look like, and what He has called You to be!

Let Him wash out all false perspectives about who You are, what You look like, and what He has called You to be!

Journal Notes

HE FORMED YOU…

Lesson Notes

You know me inside and out, You know every bone in my body; You know exactly how I was made, bit by bit, how I was sculpted from nothing into something. "Like an open book, You watched me grow from conception to birth; all the stages of my life were spread out before You, The days of my life all prepared before I'd even lived one day.

(Psalm 139:15,16 The Message)

It seems a bit repetitive doesn't it? Didn't we already cover this with the previous few verses? Do you think God might have known we would struggle with things like appearance, identity, feeling like we don't belong, and is having David head us off at the pass with this truth? Our hearts need to know there is a purpose in us being here and His intentionality concerning us speaks that there is!

> Our hearts need to know there is a purpose in us being here and His intentionality concerning us speaks that there is!

A few years ago I was learning with a group of people about the third heaven and accessing heavenly places. During that weekend as we did some activations, I had an experience that I will never forget. I was taken to heaven and given a tour. I could see things in great detail and was able to ask the angel giving me the tour any questions that I wasn't sure about like, "How come it is so bright and lovely but there are no actual lights anywhere?" At one point in this vision I walked into a large room that looked like a long library with great, big, thick, leather bound books reaching up several stories. I asked the angel what the books were and he said, "These are the chronicles of people's lives."

As I looked closer I could see a name on each binding engraved in the leather. God has brought me to that room a few times since then and once I even got to read some things that the angels were writing on the pages. All of this says your life matters! It matters to God. He took the time to weave you, mold you, shape you and write about you before you even came along!

Speak to your heart right now and tell it, "You are God's special plan. You are not a mistake or born at the wrong time or in the wrong place. You matter because you matter to God and He built you with dual purpose: to love Him with everything you have and to walk out the destiny He has for you!"

REFLECTION AND ACTIVATION

1. Just one question today:

   Daddy, what have You written in your books about me and how do I step toward what You have planned?

2. It's soaking time!

   Get comfortable (well not TOO comfortable) and go ahead and engage with God in a posture of rest. See you tomorrow…

You matter because you matter to God, and He built you with dual purpose: to love Him with everything you have and to walk out the destiny He has for you!

Journal Notes

SANDS OF THE SEA – SERIOUSLY?

God has an endless supply of wonderful thoughts about us.

Lesson Notes

Your thoughts—how rare, how beautiful! God, I'll never comprehend them! I couldn't even begin to count them — any more than I could count the sand of the sea. Oh, let me rise in the morning and live always with you! (Psalm 139:17,18 The Message)

When I look at this verse I can't help but think, "Wow, most of us can't even scrape together two or three good thoughts to think about ourselves." But God has an endless supply of wonderful thoughts about us. In fact, the word that is translated "thoughts" is actually the Hebrew word "rea" meaning thoughts and purposes. Both God's thoughts and His purposes toward you are rare and beautiful. Our minds have difficulty understanding His marvelous intentions toward us. This section of verses reminds me of Jeremiah 29:11.

"For I know the plans that I have for you," declares the LORD, "plans for welfare and not for calamity to give you a future and a hope."

(Jeremiah 29:11 NASB)

I know what I'm doing. I have it all planned out—plans to take care of you, not abandon you, plans to give you the future you hope for.

(Jeremiah 29:11 The Message)

Are you getting the message yet? No, not in your head – in your heart? You are so incredibly loved and He, Abba Father, Daddy God, Heavenly Papa, has purposes and plans to bless you, to give you a future and a hope. Our hearts respond to that kind of love with something like, "Oh God, let me be always with You!"

David finished off the Psalm with talking about how his heart knowledge of God leads him to hate sin and evil. In syncing with God's heart for Him he has synced with God's heart in general and God's dislike for everything that robs life from us. David states this understanding and fusion with God's heart with great flare. What matters to us is not how well we can express this understanding but how we live it out.

Do we embrace this truth and do we grieve for the ways we have accepted the counter of His very best for us?

REFLECTION AND ACTIVATION

David finishes the Psalm with another invitation to search his heart and life and to lead him in His ways. Let's begin where David left off…

1. Pray with me:

    "Father, investigate my life and get all the information firsthand. Lord, show me the things that grieve You and download to me the thoughts and purposes of Your heart."

2. Let's ask a few questions and then finish off the week with soaking Him in.

    a. Daddy, what are some of Your thoughts toward me that I keep missing?

    b. What purposes do You have for me in this next season?

Lord, show me the things that grieve You and reveal to me the thoughts and purposes of Your heart.

Journal Notes

THE TENDER HEART OF GOD

This teaching is often referred to as the "Mother Heart of God," as well. The majority of the revelation in this teaching has come from an incredible lady named Denise Jordan. Denise and her husband, James, are pastors and teachers who carry the Father Heart message in an incredible way. They have brought revelation and transformation to many hearts both with their anointed teachings and hugs!

One of the clearest pictures we have of the Mothering Heart of God is seen in this Scripture from Matthew 23:

> *Jerusalem! Jerusalem! Murderer of prophets! Killer of the ones who brought you God's news! How often I've ached to embrace your children, the way a hen gathers her chicks under her wings, and you wouldn't let me. (Matthew 23:37 The Message)*

In this passage, Jesus is speaking to a nation who killed the very people God sent to help them. His heart was aching for them. He still wanted to gather them in and love on them, but they would not allow themselves to be loved. Even so, the heart of God persisted toward them.

I think we often associate that kind of blind love with moms, who, no matter what the child has done, continue to believe and hope for the best. They often continue to shelter and love their children to their own detriment. In this Scripture verse the Lord is aligning Himself with a Mother's love. That may seem strange to us as we know God is not a woman, but the truth is, both the fullness of the Masculine and the Feminine are resident within the Person of God. Let's look at a couple of other verses first, before we dive into how we know that statement is true.

Jesus wanted to gather them in and love on them, but they would not allow themselves to be loved.

As a mother comforts her child, so I will comfort you. (Isaiah 66:13 NIV)

Can a mother forget the baby at her breast and have no compassion on the child she has borne? Though she may forget, I will not forget you. See I have engraved you on the palms of my hands; your walls are ever before Me. (Isaiah 49: 15,16 NIV)

Again, the Lord is referencing Himself with the visual picture of a mother – a tender, compassionate heart. This week we are going to look at the fullness of masculinity and femininity that are both resident within God. In so doing, we will also find the things resident within us that reflect Him fully.

See I have engraved you on the palms of my hands. (Isaiah 49:16)

IN HIS IMAGE...

Lesson Notes

Then God said, "Let Us make man in <u>Our image</u>, according to Our likeness; and let <u>them</u> rule over the fish of the sea and over the birds of the sky and over the cattle and over all the earth, and over every creeping thing that creeps on the earth."

<u>God created man in His own image</u>, in the image of God He created him; <u>male and female He created them</u>. (Genesis 1:26,27)

God created both male and female in His likeness and image. Therefore, both the feminine attributes and characteristics, and the male attributes and characteristics, are resident within God.

God created both male and female in His likeness and image.

You and I, no matter what gender, are made in the image of God. I am not saying God is feminine, but simply that the fullness of God encompasses both the masculine and the feminine in their most perfect and Godly form.

Since we are created in His image that also means that resident within you is both the feminine and masculine. I know the thought of this might have your head spinning, but hopefully, by the end of the week you will understand just how important it is to comprehend this in trying to understand His heart toward us. We will spend the next few days breaking this concept down and looking at what the true feminine and true masculine are meant to be like; and further, how we return to living out of these attributes.

REFLECTION AND ACTIVATION

1. Let's do a little exercise today: Without peeking ahead, write a little list under each heading about what you would think are true feminine and true masculine attributes. In the next two days you can compare your list and understanding to the teaching and see what God wants to say to you through this exercise!

2. Today's journal assignment is to fill in the lists and even ask the Holy Spirit to tell you how He sees masculine and feminine and then spend some time soaking in His wonderful Presence!

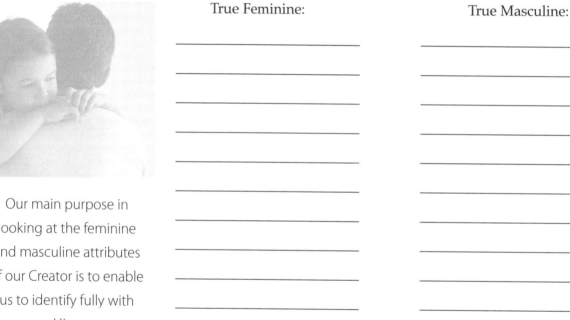

True Feminine:

True Masculine:

Our main purpose in looking at the feminine and masculine attributes of our Creator is to enable us to identify fully with Him.

Journal Notes

WHO'S THAT GIRL?

When people are in the right relationship with the Lord, operating in the true feminine includes nurturing others and bringing life to those around us.

Lesson Notes

What is the "true feminine?" It is what was resident within the Father at creation. It is what feminine was supposed to look like before the fall, recorded in Genesis, chapter three. After the fall, when sin entered the world, we encountered the false, or broken feminine. Today we are going to look at both the true and the false feminine and then spend some time examining our lives and allowing the Holy Spirit to reveal which one we are living.

Our main purpose in looking at the feminine and masculine attributes of our Creator is to enable us to identify fully with Him. Feminine and masculine attributes are found in both men and women. As you read through the following discourse on the feminine attributes of God, you will realize that men also carry these attributes although they are of the feminine nature of God. Women also carry a measure of the masculine attributes of God. The feminine and masculine attributes of God are found in both men and women. The attributes are not isolated to one gender. Every individual has a feminine and masculine side The true Feminine is the "being" side of God. It's the ability to simply "be," out of which comes the power to respond to God and to others around us in a healthy fashion. Think of Mary of Bethany who chose the one greatest thing – to "be" at the feet of Jesus. The true feminine wants to know and be known, to connect at a heart level. When people are in right relationship with the Lord, operating in the true feminine includes nurturing others and bringing life to those around us. Both wisdom and discernment flow from the true feminine part of God. In fact, in Scripture, wisdom is always spoken of in the feminine gender. The ability to rest and to trust comes from the feminine side and its ability to communicate freely with God from the heart. A person in touch with the true feminine can obey without fear and live from the heart.

So what does the false feminine look like? It can look like some of the stereotypical women we see (and yell at) on TV or in the movies – women who are over-emotional, unable to make decisions, or even take care of themselves. Due to their inability to make decisions, they tend to greet life from the victim perspective. The false feminine is helpless, needy, often filled with self-pity, and unable to take responsibility for her own life. The false feminine can often be very manipulative and controlling or on the flip side, might be easily controlled and manipulated. The false feminine may become a seducer of men or conversely bend into the image and likeness of a man.

I think we all agree which one we would rather demonstrate! When we are healed and allow God to access all the hurt places, we will demonstrate more of the true feminine and true masculine nature of God without effort. I love the description of the true feminine as wanting "to know and be known."

Most women want to communicate, which is a function from the true feminine side, and God loves to communicate with us; it's what He longs for! Let's think about this for a minute. I have two gorgeous little girls and what's remarkable about both of them is, from the very beginning they sought eye contact and tried to talk! Long before they got moving around or exploring, their demonstrated goal was to connect. Both of my girls stopped drinking when I fed them if I broke eye contact with them. And both of them prefer to cuddle and connect rather than to climb or roll around. Why? They don't have restraints on their true nature and therefore are in touch with that side of God that longs for connection! God is the Master Life Giver and Nurturer. From weaving us together in our mother's womb to marriage and having our own kids, God's love and nurture covers us and carries us through.

The ability to rest and to trust comes from the feminine side and its ability to communicate freely with God from the heart.

I love Psalm 27:10 –

Though my father and mother forsake me the Lord will receive me. (NIV)

We can trust Him to be who He says He is, and to both nurture and commune with us as well as train and empower us. That's both sides of Who He is working in us and on us. When I first heard Denise teach this, I was blown away because I realized that due to my own hurt and pain, I was living out of the false masculine (which I will explain later) instead of the false feminine. I wasn't over emotional, but rather shut down and even stoic because that is how I survived. God has so much more for us than broken existence and survival. He really does give us life and life abundantly if we would only allow Him to come in and do a little re-wiring!

REFLECTION AND ACTIVATION

1. Let's start by journaling today. I want you to ask these questions regardless of whether you are a man or a woman because you have both the masculine and the feminine side within you!

    a. Daddy, in what ways have I been operating in the false feminine? What do you want to tell me about that?

    b. I know that creativity flows out of the true feminine. In what ways have You made me creative?

2. Take some time to practice the true feminine by soaking and resting in that trust and love you have for Him.

God has so much more for us than broken existence and survival. He really does give us life and life abundantly when we allow Him to come in and do a little re-wiring!

Journal Notes

ARE YOU A MAN OR A MOUSE?

Lesson Notes

Today let's look at the true and false masculine. True Masculine is the "doing" side of God. It's the power to act, stand for truth, and initiate. I love what Denise says about this initiating: "God is so masculine that we are all feminine before Him! We cannot initiate anything; we can only receive from Him." The true masculine is the ability to give form to and call life into someone. That's what Dads are called to do with little kids – to call us to life and the fullness of it. The power to protect, defend, and to stand for truth and what is right, all flows out of the true masculine. It also contains the power and ability to prevail in the face of adversity, and to finish what was started. The masculine ways are linear, logical, rational, intellectual and observable. The true masculine tends to know about people and things rather than be known. They want to know what you are thinking and what your problems are, in order to fix them. They like to have all their ducks in a row.

I love the description of the true masculine, because I have met many men who flow in it well. Picture a scene where the wife comes home and starts to talk about a run-in she had at work and "Dum-da –da-da!" in bursts Super Male! He will now fix all your troubles and get all your ducks lined up and marching to the right tune. Then he might even rush into the office to defend and stand up for his girl! It's classic hero stuff folks, and that drive flows out of the true masculine. When Alyn and I first got together someone gave Alyn this little tip: when AJ comes home all upset about something ask her the question, "Do you want me to

The power to protect, defend, and to stand for truth and what is right, all flows out of the true masculine.

listen like a boy or listen like a girl?" If I said boy, he would help me reason my way through it, but if I said girl, he would just hold me and rub my shoulder and let me vent. I'm sure that little tidbit has helped us relate beyond measure.

True masculine is ready to "do" – to get going and get on with it! Research conducted on newborn babies shows some interesting observations. From a very early age boy babies are moving their arms and legs and no doubt planning their exploration of any given room, while girl babies are usually just moving one thing – their mouths! My friend Jo Smith and I had babies five days apart, I had a girl and she had a boy named Judah. Judah is a gorgeous little guy and started boot scooting around the house many months before my daughter, Abi, even considered it as a goal. Abi was happy to learn "tricks" as we called it, of sign language and fun communication, while Judah, at the same age, was plotting the exploration of his world! Abi didn't even bother to try and crawl until the day after she turned one. She would just watch and listen and play near the adults.

We long to be known and enjoy "knowing about," and these are both good things from God.

I also have to smile about the "knowing about" perspective, rather than "being known." In the eight years that we travelled as itinerate pastors and speakers, we would go to many nations and reside with many hosts. I noticed how the female host would talk about the people I was going to meet, while the male host would download interesting facts about the landmarks we would drive by and the place we would be visiting. That object lesson summed it up for me right there; yet with God, we know we have both resident within us. We therefore realize we long to be known and enjoy "knowing about," and these are both good things from God.

Here is a key… the true masculine can only thrive where the true feminine is operating, and vice versa. If you don't see the true feminine operating, the true masculine probably isn't resident either.

How do we recognize the false masculine? It's rugged, stoic, individualistic and independent. Think of any Clint Eastwood movie that's hard, harsh, violent, unemotional, competitive, and seeks to win at any cost, and that's what it looks like.

While society tends to value the masculine ways of doing things and the left brained, over the feminine way of being and the right brained, God is the fullness of both. He spoke into existence all that was created, and that's both doing (action) and creative, so He was flowing out of both capacities. He loves to communicate and be part of the details of our lives. He already knows all about you, but He longs to know you and be known by you.

As I previously said, I realized the first time I heard this teaching that in my woundedness, I had not morphed into the false feminine, but the false masculine. I had become a survivor and I aimed for being bulletproof. I wanted to project the image that I was strong, unstoppable and had no weakness. While those who knew me well could see past this, it was the bravado I put on for the general public. It was a mask or false strength that covered a reality of pain and brokenness. I hated weakness in myself, and therefore hated it in anyone else. I remember many times going to the movies or watching TV and the people I was with would cry, and I would admonish them with, "Oh, for crying out loud it's just a movie! Suck it up, would you!" I was very cutting and sarcastic and I used my words like weapons to keep people away. Have you done that?

REFLECTION AND ACTIVATION

1. Let's journal first again today and ask God these questions:

    a. Daddy, what am I living out of? Do I jump back and forth and if so what triggers the jump?

    b. What do you want to speak into the true masculine side of me today?

2. Spend as long as you can just letting Him wash over you with His goodness.

God loves to communicate and be part of the details of our lives. He already knows all about you, but He longs to know you and be known by you.

Journal Notes

TUPPERWARE, ANYONE?

Lesson Notes

You and I are created for love and intimacy in our families.

Today we are going to learn about something called storge love. Storge is one of the four Greek words that we translate to the English word "love." While storge doesn't appear in Scripture, it is the kind of love that would best describe this nurturing, mothering kind of love that we see in many of those verses that we looked at in the Introduction.

Let's look at all four of the words that we translate to mean love.

- **Phileo**: which means an affectionate, experiential, brotherly kind of love.

- **Agape:** which means the unconditional love of God like we learned in Week Three.

- **Eros:** is the sexual love between a man and a woman.

- **Storge:** is a gentle, compassionate and comforting love. It's family love.

You and I are created for love and intimacy in our families. Specifically, our mothers are the first people who address that need. We first experience storge or the lack thereof in the womb. If mom is excited and looking forward to having this baby, she will do things like affectionately rub her stomach and speak to the baby in quiet moments. Doing those things from the very beginning speak into the baby, "You are loved, you are wanted, it's safe out here for you." On the other hand, this child may have been conceived at a time when the parents didn't feel was great timing; or they find out it's a girl and they wanted a boy; or there are serious financial problems within the home and the pregnancy is an added point of stress; then the child can also begin to feel a love deficit in the womb. Storge love is felt and not logically explained. A baby knows if he/she is loved right from the womb. The baby can actually feel it, which makes sense since storge love must be experienced, rather than explained. For example, if a baby is crying, do you go over and speak logically to it about why it is okay, or do you pick it up and cuddle it until it comes to peace?

If mom is emotionally healthy, she will be able to place within her children the ability to receive and contain love throughout their lives. Imagine if you will, a Tupperware container right about where your diaphragm is, and its function is to catch and contain storge love so that you can head forward into life knowing you are here for a reason and that you are safe, understood and loved. Is anyone else thinking we should have a new kind of Tupperware party right now? This so-called Tupperware container is filled by receiving storge love from our moms and dads and siblings and grandparents, and all those people who God has placed here to love us.

How is storge communicated? Storge is received in three primary ways: first is affectionate touch – cuddles, hugs, tickling and playing with close tender contact. Babies love and respond to all kinds of tender touch. They want to be held and have their feet played with. They crave and need physical contact. In so doing, we start to fill their "Tupperware" container which enables them to carry and receive love throughout their lives.

The second way it is received is through loving eye contact. Babies drink in love and security through this eye contact and start receiving the messages of "I'm okay, I'm wanted." Both my girls have been eye contact cravers! They would both stop nursing if I looked away and both would settle down by being held close and getting eye contact. My littlest one, Tia, will actually arch away when you hold her to be able to look into your eyes, and is happy to just stare for ages.

If we as parents speak to our children in loving, nurturing and tender tones we begin to build their basic trust while at the same time conveying value and safety to their spirits.

The final way they receive love is through our tone of voice when talking to them. If our tone as parents or loved ones is sharp, business like or laced with frustration, that little child begins to interpret that right away. However, if we speak to them in loving, nurturing and tender tones we begin to build their basic trust while at the same time conveying value and safety to their spirits. Again, storge love is experienced – not understood.

For example, Alyn's Mom is to the Mother Heart what Bill Gates is to Microsoft. She is incredibly warm and loving to every person she meets and without anyone spelling it out for her, she meets you with affectionate touch, loving eye contact and a loving tone of voice. I think that amount of storge being poured into Alyn from a very early age is a big part of why he is so secure. Alyn is shocked if people don't like him, and he would have no idea why they wouldn't because he is so lovable. It doesn't come from a prideful place, but rather from being secure in who he is. And if you love on Alyn, he can receive it without it flowing out through his feet the moment after it's spoken.

You can see a live demonstration of storge at work if you take any cute baby out shopping or to church. What does everybody want to do? They usually reach out to touch them, either stroke their hands or pinch their cheeks (even in flu season – why, people, why?) Then they will make eye contact and lose the power of logical speech – digressing to purring and high-pitched noises and the occasional half sentence. It's hysterical, really, that such a tiny, little baby just pulled the storge right out of you!

Here's the scary part. As a parent you can provide your child with every material thing you can think of, but if you fail to cuddle and hug, or play with them and look lovingly into their eyes and speak in loving tones, you fail to give that child what it needs to survive. After WWII some reports were disclosed that shocked the medical world. In Nazi Germany during World War II, they experimented with 50 babies and took care of all their physical needs, such as feeding and changing them, but they did not speak to them or show them any affection. Within six months every baby had died. A similar result happened in London after the bombings during the same war, when the hospitals

As a parent you can provide your child with every material thing you can think of, but if you fail to provide physical expressions of storge love, you fail to give that child what it needs to survive.

were filled with orphaned children of all ages. They were placed in wards to be cared for during crisis but the nurses had no time to cuddle or comfort them and nine out of 10 children did not survive! It's shocking isn't it? Some of you reading this right now are an absolute miracle!

In fact, even as adults we need storge! Dr. James Dobson says we need 12 affectionate touches a day to remain emotionally healthy.

What happens if our mothers and families were not able to supply us with the storge we needed? For one thing, since storge awakens the true feminine within us, (which includes the ability to respond to God, to obey without fear, to be able to give away love in return) we will struggle with intimacy. If we did not grow up with warm touch, empathy and compassion can shut down emotionally.

The amazing thing with God is that there is nothing that is impossible for Him to do – and do it really well. He knows the details of your life and He knows where your life was deficient in areas, so it's actually quite an easy thing to invite Him to restore your container and enable you to give love, receive love, and walk through life knowing you are loved. Are you ready for a Tupperware party now?

The amazing thing with God is that there is nothing that is impossible for Him to do – and do it really well.

REFLECTION AND ACTIVATION

1. Here are some questions for you to journal about:

   a. Father, when people show love to me, am I able to receive it and contain it or does it flow out of my feet?

   b. Do I know I am loved and wanted at my very core?

   c. Does my Tupperware need repair or replacement?

2. If you need to, I encourage you to pray a quick prayer of forgiveness to your mom or family for not meeting your storge needs. Now go ahead and soak, but while you are doing it, place your hands on your stomach and ask the Holy Spirit to have a divine Tupperware party within – to replace or repair your storge container and enable you to receive the love that is pouring out around you!

Journal Notes

I WILL BE COMFORTED…

Lesson Notes

The first time I heard this teaching, I had a picture of a storge container that looked more like a colander than a container. I was able to see that no matter how much someone said they loved me or showed me that love, I only retained the reality of that for a few moments before it seemed to slip right out of my hands and I was back to feeling alone and unloved. In those moments I didn't even really know how to turn to God because I never received that nurturing love that teaches us how to be comforted in the first place. So, here I was walking around with a love deficit and not knowing how to let God comfort me out of it, which is when I began to look to other things for comfort.

No matter how much someone said they loved me or showed me that love, I only retained the reality of that for a few moments before it seemed to slip right out of my hands.

If we do not have a solid foundation in storge love, then we end up having trouble relating and receiving all the other types of love as well, particularly eros (sexual) love. Often, without a storge base, eros love can head into overdrive because we need to be comforted, and we will be comforted somehow. It is this dynamic that drives those with a love deficit into addictions, false affections and counterfeit comforts. Those not touched in a healthy way as a baby or toddler will often allow themselves to be touched in unhealthy ways as a teenager and adult. We are seeking to answer that cry of, "Please, someone, love me!" So we bond with whatever can make us feel better for a time.

What types of things are we talking about? Let's work through a little list of examples, and while we do, ask the Holy Spirit to reveal any place where we are turning to false comforts.

Because of the tendency to turn to eros for love, sexual issues are some of the most obvious things we turn to for comfort. Struggles with masturbation and pornography can stem from a lack of foundational love. At its root, same sex attraction can stem from a lack of storge love. Even having an insatiable need for sex can be a result.

But it's not limited to just sexual issues. People who lacked storge in their formative years can end up in one codependent relationship after another as they seek to get their love need met as adults, through a person rather than God. It doesn't matter if that person is their best friend, spouse, lover or home group leader, they will latch on and suck them dry in an attempt to get their needs met! Of course, no one person can meet those needs no matter how wonderful they are because it's a God-designed need that only He can fill! In addition, many singles fall into believing the fantasy that "When I get married all my love needs will be met," or "When I have kids they will meet that love need." This mindset is dangerous because it places irrational demands upon their spouse for fulfillment, while their children end up having to make them look good and feel loved rather than the other way around.

Perhaps we turn to escapism. It doesn't really matter if it's movies, reading, studies, work, sports, or church; it's just whatever we use other than God to fill the void. We may also fill that void with addictions to alcohol, drugs, shopping or chocolate. It's still a stuffing that will never fill the need.

Lastly, we may turn to control. We try to control our environment and control our world so we don't feel pain, or lack or shame. But walking down that path often leads to anorexia, bulimia and over eating in a vain attempt to answer a love need that was answered 2000 years ago on the cross.

As for me, I selected a healthy mix of many of those issues. Sometimes I hid in books, (primarily cheesy romance novels). I also strived

People who lacked storge in their formative years can end up in one co-dependent relationship after another in an attempt to get their needs met.

to earn attention and love by competing and excelling in many sports and alternatively starving myself in different seasons.

The good news is not only can God replace that broken storge container, but He can and will break you of every pattern of comfort you have entered into if you invite him into the midst of it.

> *Praise be to the God and Father of our Lord Jesus Christ, the Father of compassion and the God of all comfort, Who comforts us in all our troubles, so that we can comfort those in any trouble with the comfort we ourselves have received from God. (2 Corinthians 1:3,4 NIV)*

God longs to comfort you, walk you through your troubles, and heal you, if you will give Him that place.

REFLECTION AND ACTIVATION

1. My encouragement to you this day is to confess to Him any cycles of sin or self-comfort that you are trapped in and then invite Him into the midst of that pattern to break the cycle and teach your heart to receive comfort from Him.

2. Let's journal and ask these questions:

   a. Father, are there any patterns of false comfort that I have not identified yet?

   b. In which moments have You most wanted to comfort me but I wouldn't let You?

The good news is not only can God replace that broken storge container, but He can and will break you of every pattern of comfort you have entered into.

Journal Notes

CAN I KEEP IT, MOM?

Have you ever taken your child shopping when they are at that age where they are not aware enough to know that everything costs money, but they are aware enough to know that they want everything? I believe that's kind of where we are at. We are at the "Really, can I have this? Can I keep it?" stage. And the answer is yes.

So how do we keep a revelation of the Father's heart and not allow it to flow out between our toes at the first sign of trouble? There are a few practical things we can do that will help ensure this.

Recognize it costs something to keep it. If your mom let you get that cute little puppy you would have to feed it, right? Feed your new found revelation from the Word. Spend your time and energy and invest money in pursuing this revelation until you live out of the place of knowing it's true. We will be spending this week circling some foundational truths about the Father heart that you can meditate on and ingest.

Feed your new found revelation from the Word. Spend your time and energy in pursuing this revelation until you live out of the place of knowing it's true

Continue spending regular time with God even when the study is done. Ask Him to highlight for you a Rhema Word about His heart for you that can be directly written into your heart understanding.

Keep soaking and pursuing rest. It sounds funny to say pursuing rest, it almost has the visual of running after a stop sign. However, it has been said that "anything worth possessing is worth fighting for" and the same goes for a lifestyle of finding your home in Him. It is worth expending energy in planning and clearing your schedule to just "be" with Him. Not pray, read, or "do" in any way, but just be.

I think we have all had those seasons or at least watched this phenomena occur where a person leaps from one event or conference to another in an attempt to get filled, but seems to lose what God has done in between. Why? I think it's because they haven't learned to feed themselves so they starve if no one offers them a meal. Continue how you have begun with this study and allow its tools to see you through this wonderful journey that God has destined for you.

Ask God to highlight for you the truth about His heart for you that can be directly written into your heart understanding.

TASTE AND SEE

Lesson Notes

I want you to spend a few minutes thinking about the different ways God has met you in the past eleven weeks. Have you felt His Presence either like a blanket of peace or maybe like electricity while you have been soaking? Have you heard His voice answering your questions and whispering truth to your spirit? Have you felt His Presence or seen a vision of Him that has revealed His heart toward you? All of those things are experiences with Papa God.

God wants you to experience His goodness; He wants you to feel, sense, see, hear, taste, smell and touch His Presence. He is an experiential God, and what's ironic about that is much of the church is afraid of divine experience – or even worse, completely against it. God wants us to experience Him deeply, rather than relating to Him as slaves, so He went to extraordinary measures to make a way for us to be in a loving relationship with every part of the Godhead. If He didn't want to have a relationship with us, then He would have just left a list of things to do and not to do, along with the consequences thereof. It would have been every man for himself. But He didn't do that. Instead, He sent His only Son to provide a way back to relationship with Him because He loves us so much He can't stand the thought of being separated from us.

So, let's think about this whole lie that we don't need experiences with God or that He doesn't want us to have them. Consider this: the

God wants you to experience His goodness; He wants you to feel, sense, see, hear, taste, smell and touch His Presence.

whole Bible is a book of people's encounters with God. God delights in experience with us and wants us to enjoy them.

His love-plan does not include having a long distance, one-sided, letter-writing relationship with you. Would anyone sign up for that kind of relationship? He desires a two-way, experiential, talking, living, breathing, relationship with you! He wants you to know, that you know, that you know, that you know, that you are loved. He wants this truth to be established in your heart and not only your mind. He desires for you to walk through this life feeling the reality of it!

O taste and see that the LORD is good; How blessed is the man who takes refuge in Him! (Psalm 34:8)

The word "taste" in this Scripture is the Hebrew word "taam" which means to "taste" or "perceive with your senses." That certainly cannot be interpreted as non-experiential, can it? The word "see" in this verse is the Hebrew word "raah" which means to "see" or "access." God wants you to not only access Him but to see Him and what He is doing; to taste the goodness that can only be from Him. He desires you to perceive with your senses His fullness all around you!

God desires a two-way, experiential, talking, living, breathing, relationship with you! He wants you to know, that you know, that you know, that you know, that you are loved.

REFLECTION AND ACTIVATION

1. Today, use the majority of your time to connect with Him. Get comfortable and put on some soaking music and invite the Holy Spirit to come and wash over you with waves of His goodness.

2. When you are done soaking, then journal about this one question:

   a. Daddy, do you really want me to experience You? Is there anything in the way?

Journal Notes

EVERLASTING AND EXTRAVAGANT!

Lesson Notes

We are going to take a look at two verses today that solidify this message of the Father's heart for us. I love these verses as they confirm that He really does love me as much as I think He does, and more!!!!

See how great a love the Father has bestowed on us, that we would be called children of God; and such we are! (1 John 3:1)

What marvelous love the Father has extended to us! Just look at it—we're called children of God! (1 John 3:1 The Message)

God's love toward you is huge! HUGE!!! He claims you as His own and His heart full of love is always turned toward you. You are His and that is non-negotiable unless you choose to walk away; and even then you are still His. He simply waits for you to turn around and head back in His direction!

I have loved you with an everlasting love; Therefore I have drawn you with lovingkindness. (Jeremiah 31:3)

I've never quit loving you and never will. Expect love, love, and more love! (Jeremiah 31:3 The Message)

In my early years as a Christian, I would read the Bible through the lenses of my issues and come to some very false conclusions. As we learned many weeks ago, we often see God through the image of our

God's love toward you is huge! He claims you as His own and His heart full of love is always turned toward you.

own father and our relationship with him. I did that and as a result, when I read the Old Testament, I would only see the places where God was dealing with sin and never noticed any verses about His love or faithfulness! I had the crazy idea (although I am joking now) that we have the God of the Old Testament, and then we hear nothing from God for 400 years while He met with some inner healing people and sorted out some stuff, and then we have the New Testament where He is all friendly and loving!

You and I could read the same verse of Scripture and very possibly get completely different revelations from it. It's interesting how much of what we comprehend is colored by how we view things! Here we see an Old Testament verse talking about the love of God and how it is never ending! From His love in the garden at creation through to the present, He has never changed; He loves us and the Bible is a story of His pursuit of relationship with us, and our response in turn.

REFLECTION AND ACTIVATION

1. Let's journal first today and ask the following questions:

    a. Daddy, do I live like I am fully loved by You yet?

    b. What parts of me are You still trying to love back to life?

2. Grab your pillow and have a great soak. Bask in His love for you today.

From His love in the garden at creation through to the present, He has never changed; He loves us and the Bible is a story of His pursuit.

Journal Notes

CREATED FOR LOVE...

Lesson Notes

It's quite an amazing thought, really: you and I were created for no other reason than to find loving relationship with God. He created you to love and to be loved in return. He created you for a real, raw, unending and overwhelming romance with His Son for eternity. It's very difficult to wrap your mind around that kind of forethought. He planned you long before you were born, numbered your days, wrote them in His books, and waited excitedly for your birth and for the day you would turn to Him knowing you would seek Him with all of your heart and fall deeply in love with Him.

He even watched you build your walls of fear so you could protect your heart from hurt instead of turning to Him in each moment to breathe healing. He stood with arms outstretched on either side as you took your first steps in your walk with Him – ready to catch you with each wobble or fall, never getting frustrated with you no matter how long it has taken to get stable. He is not impatient for you to get it together or be perfect. He knows you, every part of you, and He loves you right now the way you are!

> *Blessed be the God and Father of our Lord Jesus Christ, who has blessed us with every spiritual blessing in the heavenly places in Christ, Just as He chose us in Him before the foundation of the world, that we would be holy and blameless before Him in love.*

You and I were created for no other reason than to find loving relationship with God. He created you to love and to be loved in return.

He predestined us to adoption as sons through Jesus Christ to Himself, according to the kind intention of His will, To the praise of the glory of His grace, which He freely bestowed on us in the Beloved. (Ephesians 1:3-6)

These verses show so amazingly how God's heart is always turned toward us. He predestined you to be adopted as His child. He is for you and not against you. He will never leave nor forsake you, He created you for relationship and He longs to see your face each day and hear your voice!

You are blessed with every spiritual blessing in heavenly places. What you need from heaven and in life is available to you as sons and daughters of God.

REFLECTION AND ACTIVATION

1. Spend some time soaking first today and then let's journal through these questions:

    a. Father, what spiritual blessings are within reach that You would like me to pursue?

    b. Father, what three steps do You want me to take to keep going deeper with You into this love that You are pouring out on me?

You are blessed with every spiritual blessing in heavenly places. What you need from heaven and in life is available to you as sons and daughters of God.

Journal Notes

DON'T FORGET…

God says you are sons and daughters, children with an inheritance, and dearly loved.

Lesson Notes

As you go forward, don't forget who you are – who God says you are! You are sons and daughters, children with an inheritance, and dearly loved. When everything hits the fan at home or it feels like life just came up and slapped you in the face, hold on to this truth:

You are His! He has not lost sight of you and He never will.

I want to remind you of some verses that you can hang onto as you walk forward in this wonderful walk with Him.

How great is the love the Father has lavished on us, that we should be called children of God! And that is what we are! (1 John 3:1 NIV)

For you did not receive a spirit that makes you a slave again to fear, but you received the Spirit of sonship. And by him we cry, "Abba, Father." The Spirit himself testifies with our spirit that we are God's children

(Romans 8:15,16 NIV)

We are His kids and He takes that seriously. As His children we don't have to be worried about what the devil is up to or be slaves to fear. Our inheritance as heirs is the freedom of sonship/daughtership and all that comes with it. We are blessed, given authority, loved and encouraged; we hear His voice, and we know His ways because we are His.

If that last paragraph doesn't quite ring true for you yet, then every-day remember this:

We have come to know and have believed the love which God has for us. God is love; and the one who abides in love abides in God, and God abides in him. (1 John 4:16)

You and I are still in that process of moving all that precious head knowledge about His love for us down that 12-18 inches to our hearts. We are replacing our "stinking thinking" with heavenly truths about Father God and we are letting our hearts catch up with His goodness. You will know that you have the message securely in your heart when you live like it's true – when you walk around everyday knowing deep within that everything is okay because you are loved, and that will never change.

REFLECTION AND ACTIVATION

1. Soak in that love today! Ask Him any questions you like and journal His response.

Our inheritance as heirs is the freedom of sonship/daughtership and all that comes with it. We are blessed, loved and encouraged; and we know His ways because we are His.

Journal Notes

HOME

Lesson Notes

Home. What do you think of when you hear that word? It will mean a different thing for each of us; for some it is positive and for some negative. Let's define it according to the use in this lesson's context:

Home is a place of rest and love; where one dwells with loved ones; where you can "let down your hair" and be yourself. It's the place where you wear track pants and get comfortable. It's the place where your favorite pillow lives!

God not only wants to make His home in you but for you to make your home in Him.

I do not ask on behalf of these alone, but for those also who believe in Me through their word; That they may all be one; even as You, Father, are in Me and I in You, that they also may be in Us, so that the world may believe that You sent Me. (John 17:20,21)

God not only wants to make His home in you but for you to make your home in Him. He wants you to crawl up on His lap and make yourself at home. It's about finding our place of peace, and recharging in the person of the Holy Spirit. It's about finding who you really are in the truth of sonship/daughtership and knowing as an heir that you can open God's refrigerator when you are hungry or His pantry when you are in need. When we live out a place of sonship/daughtership we shine Jesus wherever we go. We get so full of the presence of God that it can't help but spill out as we move through everyday life. We become carriers of the Kingdom of Love and it impacts everywhere it goes because it is what everyone is looking for.

Do yourself a favor - determine in your hearts to remain in His love. Do not allow this to just be a season in the Father's heart, but make it a lifestyle of intimacy and connection out of which everything else flows. Let your life flow out of the life He is pouring into you. Parent out of the overflow, work out of the overflow, demonstrate miracles out of the overflow; be a student, a child, a spouse, a pastor or a sales clerk out of the overflow. Keep finding your home in Him. Keep crawling up on His lap and drinking in His love for you and His truth about who you are. You will not be easily shaken if you are hearing from Him daily His words of love, truth, comfort, and even discipline.

Learn to rest. I know it's hard sometimes, but ask the Holy Spirit to help you maintain the discipline of soaking in His Presence. Tithe your time in soaking and see how much more effective you are with the time that remains!

Keep dealing with your junk and ask God to speak into your life. Pursue a life of wholeness!

REFLECTION AND ACTIVATION

1. Spend some time in Psalm 139 while asking God questions about His love for you. Journal the insights.

2. Read John 14-17 and meditate on the verses. What is God speaking to you through these verses?

3. Soak in His Love.

Keep finding your home in Him. Keep drinking in His love for you and His truth about who you are.

Journal Notes

GIVE IT AWAY

A few years ago, Alyn and I went to Birmingham, Alabama, to teach at the "Father Loves You" Conference with John and Carol Arnott. The conference was amazing and we made several friends in those few days that have become very good friends to us subsequently. Having said that, the conference and what God did during it is not the memory that stands out to me the most about that trip.

On the Sunday of the conference, Alyn and I were offered an opportunity to minster to a different group of people after lunch. We went for lunch with the rest of the team, packed our bags for a flight that evening and then loaded into a van with a few others for a one-hour drive to a youth detention facility. We were really excited as we didn't often have opportunities to minister in such facilities, but I was also a little nervous.

On the way out we prayed and decided that I would share my testimony in combination with the message of the Father Heart of God. As we loaded out of the van it was well over 90 degrees outside and we were lead toward a steal-corrugated gym. To say it was hot in the gym would be a huge understatement. They had a fan standing in one of the doors to try and circulate the air but you couldn't feel it at all from where I stood. This particular facility was primarily for young offenders who were being given a last chance before being sent through to a penitentiary. While some of the young people had checked themselves in recognizing things were headed rapidly downhill, most had been sent by the system. They sat in specific groups and answered "yes, Ma'am" with military precision when spoken to. I'm not sure if they wanted to be there or not, but I did know that God had a plan for them that day.

When Alyn got up to do a salvation call, 70 kids responded by giving their lives to the Lord.

We were in the massive, very hot gym with the youth seated down the long side of the gym on shallow bleachers. To be able to make eye contact with all the groups, I had to stand in the middle of the gym. The tricky part was that the speaker and microphone I was given didn't work. So there we are in a tin oven and I am yelling the Father heart message at them. Does the Lord have a sense of humor? I didn't think there was any possible way they were picking up what I was laying down. Screaming about the Father's love has never been the most effective form of delivery, has it? Well thankfully, God covered it and when Alyn got up to do a salvation call, 70 kids responded by giving their lives to the Lord. It was amazing but it still would not have been my preferred delivery method!

This week we are going to talk about sharing and fully walking in the message of the Father heart of God. Now that you are starting to really live out of the Father's love, how do you give it away?

Now that you are starting to really live out of the Father's love, it's time to give it away!

KEEP GROWING

Lesson Notes

Over the last three months you have begun partnering with God in a process of tearing down walls, rewriting understanding and experiencing His love for you. Don't stop. So many people think that because they have studied something or mentally understand the information, that they also have the revelation, but it's just not so. We talked many weeks ago about the process of 1 John 4:16.

For we have come to know and have believed the love which God has for us. (1 John 4:16)

We are caught up in the marvelous process of moving head knowledge to heart revelation. We are also living more and more like we are truly His, knowing He really does love us. Don't ever think you have arrived. It is in that moment of pride that you begin to take steps backward; it's just plain orphan thinking.

How precious also are Your thoughts to me, O God! How vast is the sum of them! If I should count them, they would outnumber the sand. When I awake, I am still with Thee. (Psalm 139:17-18)

You and the Father still have lots to talk about! His thoughts toward you outnumber the sands of the sea, so surely you are not finished. The Lord in His graciousness brings us through revelation in stages because he knows how much we can digest at a time. I am not over exaggerating when I say I have been hearing, digesting and resting in this message of

The Lord in His graciousness brings us through revelation in stages because he knows how much we can digest at a time.

the Father's Love for over 19 years now. Daddy God still lives up to his lesser known Hebrew name of "Jehovah Sneaky" on a regular basis to access the deep places in me that still need to know love. I promise you it will not be any different for you if you choose to remain. I said in the beginning of this book that I know people who say things like "yep, I did the Father Heart thing…I've moved on." My question remains the same, "To what?" Everything in our Christian experience is based on this truth.

A few months ago I sent a draft of this book to John and Carol to give feedback and endorse. One day we were skyping while they were going through it and they both said they planned to work through it again doing the exercises because they were getting in touch with a deeper place Father is calling them to. What I find so amazing about that is if you know them, you know they live the message; they emanate the love of the Father wherever they go. Yet they were planning to go through a study that they easily could have written in search for all that He has for them. Don't make "arriving" the goal; make "pursuit" the goal.

In the last seven years I have spent an enormous amount of time in the Song of Songs and embracing a revelation of Jesus as my bridegroom. But it has to be said that it is the wonderful Father Heart message that made me feel safe enough and open to being awakened to the revelation of the bridegroom. Let God orchestrate the journey and don't stop breathing in His transforming love as you go.

REFLECTION AND ACTIVATION

1. Spend some time reflecting on the past three months and what the Holy Spirit has been up to in your journey into the arms of Papa. Spend some time journaling and asking Him to remind you of all barriers he has taken down and the revelation He has placed within you. Take stock of what has already happened because it's only the beginning.

2. Soak for as long as you have and breathe Him in.

Don't make "arriving" the goal; make "pursuit" the goal. Let God orchestrate the journey and don't stop breathing in His transforming love as you go.

Journal Notes

BE THE MESSAGE

Lesson Notes

Jesus was the message of the Father heart of God. He radiated that love through friendship, discipleship, healing and teaching. In every word and action He radiated the love of the Father.

I want to share with you a quote that I heard Larry Randolph say recently in a meeting:

"One of the fundamental problems with prophetic ministry in North America today is that you have people speaking on behalf of God that do not know the heart of God."

I suppose that quote makes me sad because I think it's true. We want the flash gifts and the accuracy, and I understand that, but the trouble is if we don't get the message we are misrepresenting the sender.

So how do we "be" the message? We marinate in it. Get all the resources you can and spend all the time that you can just hanging out with Him. Not with an agenda or striving to "be" but just because your heart longs to get closer and stay longer.

I have heard it said many times on different occasions, "People don't catch what you say, they catch who you are." What you carry becomes obvious by what those around us catch when we don't have a chance to preach about it. I know many people, moms and dads, that so emanate the Father's love that they never have to even say a word, and the message reaches the heart of those they encounter. My heart, both for you and for myself, is that we dive so deeply into His love for us that the splash covers everyone we come in contact with.

Jesus said, "To see me is to see the Father." (John 14:9 The Message)

Jesus was the message of the Father heart of God. He radiated that love through friendship, discipleship, healing and teaching. In each and every word and action He radiated the love of the Father. I want to be in that place where I only do what I see Him doing, only say what I hear him saying, and emanate the Father's love wherever I go. It's a good life goal, isn't it? Imagine the transformation wherever we go if we "are" the message. There is no defense for true love - the mountains, your mountains and those of your friends, will melt like wax at such love.

REFLECTION AND ACTIVATION

Journal and ask God these questions:

1. Father, what are some practical ways I can learn to just be?

2. Are there people around me that are good at just being the message?

3. Who have you placed around me that I can "be" the message to?

Let's finish by soaking. The best way to really "be" is to soak Him in again and again until you start spilling out love wherever you go.

There is no defense for true love - the mountains, your mountains and those of your friends, will melt like wax at such love.

Journal Notes

LOVE IS BEST FELT, NOT "TELT"
– I know it's not good English but it rhymes!

Lesson Notes

Now that you are "being" the message, give away what you have, and you will receive more. Look for practical ways to represent the Father's heart toward others. Be His arms, His mouthpiece or even His wallet toward those that He highlights to you.

The course of my life was changed many years ago by the faithfulness of three men who lived the Father heart message and intentionally loved a broken kid back to life. They were faithful, persistent and gracious to an often confused, wounded, reactionary and frightened girl who didn't know what to do with love when it was offered. God began wooing me to His Fathering heart using these men and their wives and then deepened that tapestry of love through the lives of many more leaders and friends who called me to life in Him. I had no choice left but surrender. Now you can be the vessel that helps bring life and hope to the people He sends across your path.

Heidi Baker talks about stopping for the one. In the midst of all of our busyness, look for the one. It may be a brief moment of giving Him away or a season where your life intersects with a life that needs Him. Don't preach; be.

Remember the Samaritan woman at the well in John chapter 4? Jesus demonstrated the love of the Father perfectly in that moment. He

Now that you are "being" the message, give away what you have and you will receive more. Look for practical ways to represent the Father's heart toward others.

spoke to her situation without condemnation for her current lifestyle and He brought hope and life.

The Lord GOD has given Me the tongue of disciples, That I may know how to sustain the weary one with a word. He awakens Me morning by morning, He awakens My ear to listen as a disciple. (Isaiah 50:4)

We are all disciples; students of a message of love. My prayer for us all is that He would awaken us each morning with a word, a message of hope and love for those that He sends across our path.

REFLECTION AND ACTIVATION

Let's do things in reverse order today! Spend 20 or 30 minutes soaking in His presence and getting filled up with love.

Ok, this next step you could do a few different ways depending on what today looks like for you.

My prayer for us all is that He would awaken us each morning with a message of hope and love for those that He sends across our path.

1. If you are able, grab your journal or some paper and go have a coffee somewhere. While you are there, ask the Lord for a word to sustain the weary and ask Him to highlight someone to you. Now ask him for an encouraging word and write it down. When you are done bring them the written encouragement and explain (without being super spiritual or freaky in any way) that you are learning to hear God's voice and felt He wanted to encourage them with a little note. Now please remember; in this moment you are either representing or misrepresenting the Father to this person so please be careful to be encouraging, uplifting and positive.

But one who prophesies is helping others grow in the Lord, encouraging and comforting them. (1 Corinthians 14:3 NLT)

2. If you are not able to get out of the house at the moment, spend some time journaling and ask the Lord for a word of encouragement for someone you will come across today. Write it down and stick it in your pocket so you have it with you. When the Lord shows you who to give it to, explain that you are learning to hear God voice and you felt He had a little message for them. Then leave them to read it.

Journal Notes

HAVE YOU SEEN MY DAD?

Whether we are on a quest to find a spiritual dad or endeavoring to be one, there needs to be lots of grace involved as none of us have arrived at perfection.

Lesson Notes

Many people are on a search for spiritual parents and that's a good thing. What is a spiritual father? How do I find one, and how do I be one? How far along do I need to be to father someone else in the message?

First of all, we need to reiterate that there are no perfect dads, not even one! Whether we are on a quest to find a spiritual dad or endeavoring to be one, there needs to be lots of grace involved as none of us have arrived at perfection. I would encourage you that it's difficult to be a spiritual parent without having allowed yourself to be parented well by one in the first place. Therefore, let's define both what we are looking for and what we desire to be, because the job description is the same:

- Emotionally and spiritually healthy parents, desire for their ceiling to be your floor. They truly want to see you succeed more than they desire success for themselves.

- They are not controlling or manipulative, and they don't play head games.

- They make room for you to grow in your areas of gifting and they are there to dust you off when you fall and stand you back up again.

- They are genuine people that do not hide their own weaknesses and appear to have no problems. They allow you to learn as they learn in life.

- They have their life and energies distributed in a healthy order and prioritize God and family above work or ministry.

I have two beautiful little girls and I want the world for them. I certainly don't want them to only get as far as I have. I desire so much more for them and I will help them get there! While seeking wisdom on their behalf I will open any doors I can for them, encourage them and make room for them to stretch their wings. My life as a parent is not about my life anymore, it's about theirs. That is the job that God has entrusted me with; raising them to walk in the fullness of all that He has for them and it's the most important job I have.

Do you want to be a spiritual dad or mom? Do that! Spend your life raising up the next generation and helping them get where they are supposed to go. You may do that in small ways and large ways. For some you will be in their lives for just a season and for others a life time. Be faithful to encourage and ask God for all the wisdom you need in regards to them. He created them, so who knows them better?

REFLECTION AND ACTIVATION

Grab your journal and let's ask the Lord some questions.

1. Father, who are the people in my life that you have sent to parent me in a healthy way? Am I letting them?

2. Are there any lessons that my heart has learned through negative spiritual Fathering that you would like to erase? (May be a good moment to release forgiveness if the Lord highlights anyone specific.)

3. Are there any opportunities for me to begin to parent someone else around me and make room for them to see their callings fulfilled?

Do you want to be a spiritual dad or mom? Spend your life raising up the next generation and helping them get where they are supposed to go.

Now spend some time soaking in His Presence again and getting ready to give it away. Remember, it's an upside down kingdom which mean to keep something you have to give it away!

Journal Notes

_____

_____

_____

_____

_____

_____

_____

_____

_____

_____

_____

_____

_____

_____

_____

_____

_____

_____

_____

_____

_____

_____

STAYING IN SONSHIP/DAUGHTERSHIP

Lesson Notes

So how do we stay in a place of Sonship or Daughtership? Keep laying down your life for the ones God has asked you to serve. Don't worry about how to build your ministry or plan strategies for your advancement, just serve faithfully. If your Spiritual Parents are the kind of people we talked about yesterday they will be throwing doors open for you that you could never open on your own.

Enjoy being a son or daughter and furthering the mission of the ones you are serving. And remember, you will reap what you sow! If you love and serve well you will find that as God promotes you others will come around you and love and serve you well! However, if you choose to grumble or connive your way into a position do not be surprised when the same things happen to you!

Paul said "emulate me as I emulate Christ." Do you as a leader want more little "yous" around? No? Well keep dealing with your stuff and letting God define and redefine you. I am not convinced that we ever arrive at perfection but I am determined to live a life that is fully accessible for healing while pursuing God's Kingdom and His plans with all that I have within me.

I am determined to live a life that is fully accessible for healing - while pursuing God's Kingdom and His plans with all that I have within me.

REFLECTION AND ACTIVATION

Grab your Journal and let's ask a few questions:

1. Are there any places in my heart that still need a revelation of sonship/daughtership?

2. Are there any practical ways that I can serve those that are trying to care for me?

3. We have now arrived at the final soaking time of this study. Hopefully, it won't be your final soaking and journaling time but just the beginning of your one-on-one private times with the Lord.

Journal Notes

_____

_____

_____

_____

_____

_____

_____

_____

_____

_____

_____

_____

_____

_____

_____

_____

_____

Journal Notes

Journal Notes

RESOURCES:

Books:

The Importance of Forgiveness by *John Arnott*

Spiritual Slavery to Spiritual Sonship by *Jack Frost*

Experiencing Father's Embrace by *Jack Frost*

How to Hear God's Voice by *Mark & Patti Virkler*

Restoring the Foundations: An Integrated Approach to Healing Ministry by *Chester & Betsy Kylstra*

The Return of the Prodigal Son: A Story of Homecoming by *Henri J. M. Nouwen*

Soaking CDs:

Home by *Laura Woodley Osman*

In Love by *Laura Woodley Osman*

The Father Sings by *Alberto & Kimberly Rivera*

Draw Near by *Alberto & Kimberly Rivera*

Captured by *Alberto & Kimberly Rivera*

Audio CDs:

Finding Father by *AJ Jones*

The Biblical Revelation of Father by *James Jordan*

The Motherheart of God the Father by *Denise Jordan*

Teaching DVDs:

Finding Father by *AJ Jones*

Father Types by *Alyn Jones*

The Tender Heart of God by *AJ Jones*

Orphans to Sons by *Alyn Jones*

Opening our Hearts to Father by *James Jordan*

Websites:

John & Carol Arnott – johnandcarol.org

Alyn & AJ Jones – catalysthome.org

Chester & Betsy Kylstra – restoringyourlife.org

Mark & Patti Virkler – cwgministries.org

James & Denise Jordan – fatherheart.net

Jack & Trisha Frost – shilohplace.org

Alberto & Kimberly Rivera – rainingpresence.com

To order copies of *Finding Father* and to learn more about Alyn and AJ Jones' ministry and itinerary, please visit www.catalysthome.org

You may also order copies of *Finding Father* and other books from XP Publishing at the store at XPmedia.com.

BULK ORDERS: We offer bulk/wholesale prices for stores and ministries. Please contact: usaresource@xpmedia.com. For Canadian bulk orders please contact:resource@xpmedia.com

XPpublishing.com
A ministry of Christian Services Association